It's another Quality Book from CGP

This book is for anyone studying OCR GCSE Food Technology.

Let's face it, D&T is pretty hard-going — you've got a whole load of technical stuff to learn on top of doing your project.

Happily this CGP book helps to take the headache out of all that learning. We've explained all the technical stuff — and drawn plenty of pictures to make the whole thing that bit clearer. Plus we've stuck in some handy hints to help make your project a winner, and some tips on exam technique.

And in true CGP style it's got some daft bits in to try and make the whole experience at least vaguely entertaining for you.

What CGP is all about

Our sole aim here at CGP is to produce the highest quality books — carefully written, immaculately presented and dangerously close to being funny.

Then we work our socks off to get them out to you — at the cheapest possible prices.

Contents

SECTION FOUR — THE DESIGN PROCESS

SECTION FIVE — PRODUCTION PROCESSES

Published by CGP

Editors:
Charlotte Burrows, Katherine Craig, Ben Fletcher, Rosie Gillham, Helena Hayes, David Hickinson,
Sarah Hilton, Ali Palin, Ed Robinson, Caley Simpson, Julie Wakeling, Sarah Williams

Contributors:
Angela Nugent, Jane Towle

With thanks to Phillip Holton for the content review.
With thanks to Gemma Hallam, Sharon Keeley and Glenn Rogers for the proofreading.

With thanks to Laura Stoney for the copyright research.

ISBN: 978 1 84762 357 7

Groovy website: www.cgpbooks.co.uk
Jolly bits of clipart from CorelDRAW®

© Crown copyright material on page 26 is produced with the permission of the Controller of HMSO
and Queen's Printer for Scotland.

Every effort has been made to locate copyright holders and obtain permission to reproduce sources.
For those sources where it has been difficult to trace the originator of the work, we would be grateful for
information. If any copyright holder would like us to make an amendment to the acknowledgements,
please notify us and we will gladly update the book at the next reprint. Thank you.

Printed by Elanders Ltd, Newcastle upon Tyne.

Based on the classic CGP style created by Richard Parsons.

Photocopying – it's dull, grey and sometimes a bit naughty. Luckily, it's dead cheap, easy and
quick to order more copies of this book from CGP – just call us on 0870 750 1242. Phew!

Text, design, layout and original illustrations © Coordination Group Publications Ltd. (CGP) 2009
All rights reserved.

Project Advice

Unlike most subjects, in **Food Technology** you actually get to <u>make something tasty</u> (well, hopefully).

The Projects are Worth 60% of your GCSE

1) Your Food Technology <u>projects</u> are called '<u>controlled assessments</u>'.

2) There are <u>two projects</u> — the first one is about making a <u>prototype</u> and the other one is about <u>designing and manufacturing</u> a product. Each project is worth <u>60 marks</u>.

3) Your teacher will give you as much help as they're allowed to by the exam board, so do <u>ask them</u>... but mostly it's <u>up to you</u> to make a <u>good job</u> of your projects.

4) You can dip into this book for a bit of extra help. Section 4 is all about the design process, so if you're not sure <u>where to start</u>, that might be a good place to look.

5) If you're wondering about a particular <u>detail</u> — what type of <u>sugar</u> to use, say — it's probably quickest to look that up in the <u>index</u> and go straight to that page.

The Exam Board Sets the Themes

You'll be given a range of <u>themes</u> and <u>starting points</u> to choose from for both of your projects.

> **For example:** A multicultural food product that will appeal to an identified target group.

You've got to pick two <u>different themes</u> though, for the two different projects.

Only Put Relevant Stuff in Your Folder

1) You'll need to produce a <u>folder</u> of evidence with all your work in for the two projects.

2) Your <u>teacher</u> will give you plenty of guidance on what needs to go in your folder, but you can use this section of the book for a <u>reminder</u>.

3) The next two pages tell you <u>what you can get marks for</u> and give you a few tips on <u>how</u> to get them.

4) Include plenty of <u>detail</u> — but don't <u>waffle</u> and don't waste space on <u>irrelevant</u> stuff.

Include Plenty of Photos

1) <u>DO</u> put in lots of <u>photos</u>. You **MUST** take photos of your final product (of course). Even the best-looking, most delicious-tasting toad-in-the-hole salad with lard vinaigrette will be reduced to a <u>foul-smelling puddle</u> if you keep it till the moderator gets round to marking your work.

2) But also take photos while you're <u>developing</u> your design (see next page)...

3) ...and during the <u>intermediate stages</u> of making your product, to show the making process:

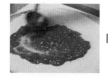    

| Add the puree to the pizza base | Sprinkle on grated cheese | Add toppings | Put in the oven | Remove from the oven and slice |

Controlled Assessment — nope, it's not funny...

Most of the controlled assessment marks depend on the <u>sheer brilliance</u> of your <u>folder</u>, so don't worry if you're not the next Nigella — you get loads of marks for <u>explaining</u> what you're doing (or trying to do).

Project Advice

The first project needs to show the moderator how you've got from the starting point to your prototype.

Cultural Understanding is Worth 5 Marks

1) Show that you understand how cultural differences affect the designing and making of food products, and the range of products available — e.g. ingredients, different methods of cooking, how food is presented.

2) Show that you know how different food products can help people to lead a healthy lifestyle — e.g. freshly-made products are generally healthier than ready meals. (There's lots about this on pages 30-31.)

Creativity is Worth 5 Marks

1) Research and evaluate existing products — visit shops to research ingredients, get ideas from recipe books.

2) Identify and research your target market — find out what they like and need, so will be more likely to buy.

3) Think about how social, moral and environmental issues link into your design process — see Section 3.

4) Analyse your research — summarise your findings and say how they'll influence your design.

5) Write a design brief (see page 44).

Designing is Worth 14 Marks

1) Write a design specification (see pages 48-49) — based on your design brief and research analysis.

2) Come up with a range of creative and original ideas to meet your design specification.

3) Record your design ideas — it's a good idea to use ICT to clearly show all aspects of your design, to work out the nutritional value of your product or just to make sure your design looks neat and well-presented.

4) Produce a detailed product specification for your prototype — include all the quality control checks too.

5) Model your design and make improvements — remember to take photos of the various things you try out.

6) Test out your ideas, taking other people's opinions into account — use sensory analysis testing, questionnaires, interviews, etc. (see pages 45 & 47). Remember to always record your results.

7) Choose your best design idea — the one that most closely matches the design specification.

Making is Worth 28 Marks

1) Organise yourself well — produce a flowchart to show the order of tasks.

2) Use the most appropriate ingredients and equipment — think about whether they're sustainable or not.

3) Work safely and hygienically — use the quality control checks from your product specification.

4) Work accurately and skilfully, using the right techniques and tools for the job — use CAM if appropriate.

5) Include lots of detail about how nutritious your product is — and how you could make it even more healthy.

Evaluating is Worth 8 Marks

1) Test and evaluate your prototype — refer back to the design specification and product specification.

2) Present your results clearly and concisely in a table, graph or chart — use a computer to help you.

3) Your prototype is unlikely to be perfect, so you should suggest some improvements you could make.

4) Use specialist terms (the glossary on pages 71-75 might help you here).

5) Double check your spelling, grammar and punctuation to make sure you don't lose out on marks.

Tell the story of your design — and give it a happy ending...

You'd scarcely believe how much moderators hate wading through pages and pages of recipes that you've copied off the internet. So do all your research — and then develop your own original ideas.

Project Advice

Your second project needs to show in detail how you've <u>designed</u> and <u>manufactured</u> a product.
The marks you get are pretty similar to the first project — but there's more focus on your <u>final product</u>.

Designing is Worth 16 Marks

1) Produce a detailed <u>design specification</u>.
2) Come up with a range of creative <u>design ideas</u> and <u>record</u> them.
3) <u>Evaluate</u> your design ideas and <u>choose</u> the best one.
4) <u>Model</u> your design, <u>trial</u> it and make appropriate <u>improvements</u>.

Final Product Info is Worth 12 Marks

1) Explain <u>why</u> you've chosen to use particular ingredients and equipment.
2) Produce a detailed <u>product specification</u>.
3) <u>Plan</u> your time well, using flowcharts (and Gantt charts if you like) to help you.

Making is Worth 24 Marks

1) <u>Organise</u> your activities in the kitchen.
2) Use the <u>most appropriate</u> ingredients and equipment.
3) Work <u>skilfully</u>, <u>safely</u> and <u>hygienically</u>. Don't be slapdash — it'll show.
4) Remember to take lots of <u>photos</u>, especially of your final product
   — use finishing techniques to make it look nice and pretty (see page 25).

Ah, a beautifully presented cuppa...

Evaluating is Worth 8 Marks

Don't just use star diagrams (page 47). Moderators see those all the time and they get a bit <u>bored</u> of them.

1) Do some serious <u>testing</u> of your product and <u>present</u> your results.
2) <u>Critically evaluate</u> your finished product (pick out good and bad points)
   — what went well? What would you change and why?
3) Make sure you <u>explain things clearly</u> — get someone who knows nothing about your project to read it and see if it makes sense.
4) Moderators love it when you use the right <u>technical words</u>
   — they love it even more when you spell them correctly.

But Don't Forget The Exams — They're Worth 40%

1) There are <u>two exams</u> where you'll be tested on <u>everything</u> you've learned during the course — materials, tools, how to design things, how to make things, health and safety, environmental issues...
2) This book can help you <u>learn all that stuff</u> — and it has <u>questions</u> for you to <u>check</u> what you know.
3) There's a <u>glossary</u> at the back of the book, in case you need to sort out your food miles from your danger zone.
4) The <u>exam technique</u> section (pages 66-69) has some <u>worked examples</u> of exam-style questions, and some hints on how to make sure you get <u>top marks</u>.

Evaluate, evaluate, evaluate...

When you evaluate a design or product, remember to explain <u>which aspects</u> of the design or product need changing and <u>why</u>. It's another little step on the long and winding road to project heaven.

Proteins

Meat, poultry and fish provide <u>high-grade protein</u> and other essential nutrients. But <u>bacteria</u> also like them, so you have to be really <u>careful</u> when buying, storing, preparing or cooking them.

Protein is Needed for *Growth and Repair*

1) Protein helps our bodies to build and repair <u>muscles</u>, <u>tissues</u> and <u>organs</u>, and helps children <u>grow</u>.

2) Protein is made of <u>amino acids</u>. Your body can make some amino acids but not others. You have to <u>eat</u> the amino acids that your body can't make — the <u>essential amino acids</u>.

> Some proteins (e.g. meat, fish, eggs, milk and soya beans) contain <u>all</u> the essential amino acids.
>
> Other proteins (e.g. peas, lentils, nuts and most beans) only contain <u>some</u> of the essential amino acids, so it's important to eat a wide <u>variety</u> of these foods. (This is particularly true for vegans — see p28.)

3) When you eat protein, your body breaks it down into amino acids and uses these to <u>build new proteins</u> — which your body then uses to make muscle, etc.

There are *Three Main Types of Meat Eaten in the UK...*

<u>Beef</u> and <u>lamb</u> have loads of B vitamins and minerals like iron and zinc.

<u>Pork</u> contains lots of thiamin (vitamin B1) and niacin (B3).

1) These are called <u>red meats</u> (though pork is sometimes classed as white meat). They're all great sources of <u>protein</u>, but too much can cause problems like <u>heart disease</u> — they're high in <u>saturated fat</u> and <u>cholesterol</u> (see p8), which clogs up your arteries.

2) Meat can be <u>tenderised</u> to make it, well... more tender. You have to partly <u>break down</u> the <u>fibres</u> in the meat. You can do this by <u>bashing it with a mallet</u>, marinating it in something <u>acidic</u> or cooking it really <u>slowly</u> (this is what makes casseroles lovely and tender).

3) Meat can <u>dry out</u> during cooking. To avoid this you can <u>baste</u> the outside of the meat with fat.

4) Once cooked, meat should be left to <u>stand</u> for a little while before serving — this lets it <u>reabsorb</u> some of the <u>juices</u> that were released in cooking.

...*Three Main Types of Poultry...*

Chicken

Turkey

Duck

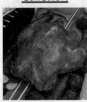 

These are <u>white meats</u> — though duck's often called red meat. *(Zeesh, you'd think someone could just <u>decide</u>.)*

Poultry is a good source of <u>protein</u> and <u>B vitamins</u> and is fairly low in <u>saturated fat</u> (especially without the skin). But it can be contaminated with <u>salmonella</u> bacteria, which can make you seriously ill — so you have to make sure it's <u>thoroughly cooked</u> before serving.

That youth's no amateur — he's a pro-teen...

Sure, meat's got protein in it, but it contains other stuff as well — e.g. red meat has loads of <u>iron</u>, and liver has loads of <u>vitamins</u>. But the tastiest meat also has lots and lots of <u>saturated fat</u>. Shame.

Proteins

...and Three Main Types of Fish

Oily fish, e.g. herring,
mackerel, salmon, tuna.

White fish, e.g. cod,
haddock, plaice, skate.

Shellfish, e.g. crab,
lobster, mussels.

Honestly, I'm not
trying to get
you drunk.

Fish is very nutritious — it contains loads of vitamins, plus omega 3 oils, which are dead good for you.

There are Now Loads of Meat Replacements

1) Vegetarians don't eat meat, so they need to get their protein and other nutrients from elsewhere. Beans, lentils and nuts are all good sources of protein, as are eggs (see p14).

2) These days, there are lots of alternative protein foods, such as:
   Tofu — made from soya beans.
   TVP (Textured Vegetable Protein) — also made from soya beans.
   Quorn™ — made from a mushroom-like fungus and egg white.

3) These products can be prepared in lots of ways, sometimes to look like meat or chicken:
   - TVP can be made into sausages, burgers and ready meals.
   - Tofu is usually just stir-fried, but it can also be used in desserts.
   - Quorn™ is more often used where you'd normally use chicken, and is available as chunks (e.g. for stir fries), mince (e.g. for chilli) or fillets (e.g. to serve in sauces).

4) These meat replacements usually don't taste of much, so they're often flavoured. One way of doing this is by marinating them (soaking them in things like oil, wine, vinegar and herbs) before cooking.

5) TVP, tofu and Quorn™ all contain the essential amino acids and are high in iron. They also contain other nutrients:

   See p16 for ways of preparing alternative protein foods.

   - TVP is high in calcium and magnesium.
   - Tofu contains a lot of B vitamins and calcium.
   - Quorn™ is high in fibre.

Practice Questions

1) What do we need proteins for?

2) List three examples of foods that contain all the essential amino acids.

3) Name two vitamins or minerals that are contained in each of the following:
   a) beef
   b) pork

4) Mary is going to cook steak for dinner. Before she fries it, she bashes it with a mallet. Explain why she does this.

5) Give one reason why eating white meat is better for you than eating red meat.

6) What are the three main types of fish? Give an example for each type.

7) Give three examples of alternative protein foods.

Section One — Types of Food

Carbohydrates

Carbohydrates are one of the major food groups. Get your teeth into this...

Carbohydrates are Needed for Energy

Carbohydrates are split into three types: sugar, starch and fibre.

SUGAR

Includes simple sugars like glucose and fructose, as well as double sugars such as lactose and sucrose. They're easier to digest than starch.

Here's some sciency mumbo-jumbo — it's all to do with the chemical structure:
- simple sugars = monosaccharides (the most basic sugar molecules)
- double sugars = disaccharides (made up of 2 monosaccharides)
- complex sugars = polysaccharides
- fibres = non-starch polysaccharides.

STARCH

Starch is a complex sugar. It needs to be broken down by digestion before the energy can be used. That's why it's good to eat starchy foods like pasta and rice a few hours before playing loads of sport, where a slow release of energy can improve performance.

FIBRE

Fibre is a type of carbohydrate that isn't digested or absorbed by the body. There's more on fibre on p9.

Several Types of Sugar are Used in Home Baking

1) Granulated sugar is for general kitchen use, e.g. to sweeten tea or breakfast cereal.

2) Caster sugar has finer crystals than granulated sugar. It's used for baking, especially cakes and biscuits, which need to have a fine texture.

3) Brown sugars — demerara and muscovado are brown sugars with strong, distinctive flavours. These are used in rich fruit cakes, gingerbread and Christmas puddings.

4) Icing sugar is a white, powdery sugar used for icing and sweets.

Most of these originally come from sugar cane. Sugar also naturally occurs in things like fruit and honey. Sugar substitutes (such as artificial sweeteners) can be used instead. They're better for your teeth and contain fewer calories than sugar

Sugar is Used in Loads of Food Products

Sugar is used widely in food manufacturing, even in savoury products. Just look on some ingredients labels — fructose, dextrose, sucrose, inverted sugar, maltose, lactose and glucose are all sugars. Sugar has lots of functions:

My god! This stuff's everywhere... Help me somebody... help!

1) It makes things sweet (obviously) or 'softens' very sharp flavours, e.g. in lemony desserts.

2) It acts as a preservative, e.g. in jam.

3) In creamed mixtures, sugar is beaten with fat, which aerates the mixture (adds air to it) and helps lighten it, e.g. in cakes.

4) It speeds up fermentation, e.g. in bread.

5) Sugar adds colour, e.g. in cakes, biscuits and pastries.

6) Sugar can be heated until it becomes a sweet-tasting, brownish liquid — this is called caramelisation. It's used to top off desserts.

My parrot loves starch — she's called Polly Saccharide...

Sugar is obviously good in some ways — it tastes great, and you get sweets, cakes, biscuits, chocolates and all things good from it. But it rots your teeth. Though I don't miss mine *that* much.

Carbohydrates

Starch can alter the Structure of Foods

STARCH IS USED AS A BULKING AGENT

Starch granules swell when a liquid is added, and so can provide the bulk of a product, e.g. the starch in flour makes up most of the volume of pasta.

STARCH IS USED AS A GELLING AGENT

When moisture is added to starch granules and heat is applied, the starch granules begin to absorb the liquid and swell. At 80 °C the starch particles break open, making the mixture thick and viscous. This is gelatinisation — it's completed when the liquid reaches 100 °C. The thickened liquid forms a gel. On cooling, the gel solidifies and takes the form of the container it's in.

STARCH IS USED AS A THICKENING AGENT

Sauces and gravies are often made using starch (in flour) and liquid. The thickness depends on the proportions of starch and liquid. When the starch and liquid are mixed together, the starch particles form a suspension — they don't dissolve. The mixture is stirred to keep the particles suspended. When heat is applied, gelatinisation occurs — this causes thickening.

STARCH IS USED IN MANUFACTURED PRODUCTS

Modified starch is used to thicken things like instant desserts, whipped cream, yoghurts and packet soup. Usually a liquid is added to the starch and it is stirred or whisked.

Modified Starches are Called Smart Starches

Modified starches (or smart starches) have been treated so they react in a particular way in certain conditions. They're often used in industrial production to improve certain qualities of food (e.g. taste, ease of use etc.).

Smart starches are a smart material — see p57 for more on them.

1) Pre-gelatinised starch thickens instantly when mixed with hot water, e.g. packet custard, instant noodles.

2) Some starches allow products to be reheated with no coagulation (becoming more solid). This is handy with frozen foods (e.g. lasagne) so they keep their moisture and nutrients when they're cooked.

EXAM TIP
The functions of different nutrients comes up all the time in the exam — so make sure you know what each one does.

3) Acid can stop normal starches from working properly. Some modified starches are immune to it, so they can be used to thicken acidic products, e.g. salad cream, which contains vinegar.

Practice Questions

1) Name the three types of carbohydrate.

2) Name four types of sugar and give one use of each one.

3) Explain why sugar is used in the following foods:
   a) jam
   b) bread
   c) biscuits

4) Describe two different uses of starch.

5) What's another name for modified starches?

Fats, Fibre and Water

Ah, now we're talking — good old-fashioned <u>fats</u> and <u>oils</u>.

There are Six Main Types of Fats and Oils

"Oi, hands off!"

1) <u>Butter</u> is made from churning cream.
2) <u>Margarine</u> is made from vegetable oils blended with a load of other stuff (which might include starch, water etc.)
3) <u>Lard</u> is made from pig fat.
4) <u>Suet</u> is made from the fat which protects animals' vital organs.
5) <u>Oils</u> come from pressed seeds (e.g. rapeseed, sunflower seed).
6) <u>Low-fat spreads</u> are mixtures of vegetable oils and water.

They're Used Loads in Pastries and Biscuits

<u>Adding flavour</u> — butter in shortbread and pastry makes them taste fantastic.

<u>Shortening</u> — rubbing fat into flour prevents gluten sticking and makes pastry and biscuits 'short' — so they're a bit crumbly.

<u>Adding colour</u> — butter in pastry makes it golden yellow.

Fats and oils are used in other products too, in lots of different ways:

- <u>Cooking</u> — deep frying (e.g. fish and chips) and shallow frying (e.g. eggs).
- <u>Enriching</u> — adding butter or cream to a sauce thickens it and makes it taste better.

Fats have Some Nutritional Value

1) Fats are a concentrated source of <u>energy</u>, as well as a source of <u>vitamins A, D and E</u>.
2) Fats provide certain <u>fatty acids</u> which are essential to the structure and function of body cells.
3) Fat provides <u>insulation</u> and helps the body <u>stay warm</u>.
4) There are <u>two types</u> of fats:

<u>Saturated fats</u> are <u>bad</u> for you. They come mainly from <u>animal</u> sources (e.g. meat, butter, suet, dripping, lard) and are <u>solid</u> or semi-solid at room temperature. They're often associated with high amounts of <u>cholesterol</u> — see below.

<u>Unsaturated fats</u> are <u>good</u> for your health. They come mostly from vegetable sources and are usually oils — they're <u>liquid</u> at room temperature. The main oils used in cooking are peanut, sunflower, corn, rapeseed and olive oil.

5) Our bodies use fat to make <u>cholesterol</u>, which is an <u>essential</u> part of all <u>cell membranes</u>. It's also needed to make some <u>hormones</u>.
6) Too much <u>saturated fat</u> increases your cholesterol levels, which can increase the risk of <u>heart disease</u>.

Lard... suet... dripping... Mmmm... that sounds real good...

<u>Processed foods</u> (see p34) can contain *loads* of fat, so it's worth checking out the alternatives. We all need a certain amount of fat in our diets, although the <u>type</u> of fat is very important.

Fats, Fibre and Water

*Fibre **Isn't** Digested by the Body*

1) Fibre is a type of carbohydrate (see p6) — it's sometimes called roughage. It helps to keep your digestive system working properly and keeps food moving through it.

2) It's found in things like:

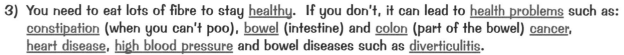

- vegetables — e.g. peas, beans, potatoes, broccoli, carrots.
- fruit and fruit juice — raspberries, prunes, bananas, apples.
- brown bread.
- wholemeal or whole grain foods — e.g. wholemeal bread, rice, pasta and flour.
- lentils, beans, seeds and nuts.

3) You need to eat lots of fibre to stay healthy. If you don't, it can lead to health problems such as: constipation (when you can't poo), bowel (intestine) and colon (part of the bowel) cancer, heart disease, high blood pressure and bowel diseases such as diverticulitis.

4) There are two types of fibre, and you need to eat both to have a healthy diet:

SOLUBLE — dissolves in water. It absorbs water as it passes through the body and it can be used and changed into other products by bacteria in the bowel. It's found in peas, root vegetables (like potatoes and carrots), fruit and oats.

INSOLUBLE — won't dissolve in water. This type of fibre passes through the body without changing at all. It's found in the skins of fruit and potatoes, whole grain and wholemeal foods, nuts and seeds.

You Can't Live Without Water

1) Around 75% of your body is water and all your body's chemical reactions and processes (e.g. digestion, excretion) take place using water.

2) You get water from drinks like water (obviously), fruit juice, tea, coffee, lemonade... Water's also found in food — vegetables and fruit contain quite a lot, and even things like meat and bread contain water.

3) If you don't have enough water from drinks and food you can become dehydrated — your body can't work properly. At first, you feel thirsty and produce less urine, and then you can get headaches or feel faint. Eventually, you can get cramp in your muscles and your blood pressure will drop. In extreme cases you can fall unconscious, go delirious and even die.

4) You should have about 2 litres of water a day — but if you're hot or exercising you need to drink more to get enough water into your system. People sometimes eat salty snacks with water or have isotonic drinks — this helps more water be absorbed by the body instead of it just passing straight through. They also help replace nutrients that are lost through dehydration.

Practice Questions

1) List six types of fats and oils, and describe briefly how each is made.

2) Describe three functions of fats and oils in making pastry.

3) a) What's the difference between saturated and unsaturated fats?
   b) Give two examples of each.
   c) Which is more closely linked with cholesterol — saturated or unsaturated fat?

4) Name four foods that are a good source of fibre.

5) What are the two different types of fibre?

6) What can happen if you get dehydrated?

7) Say "cholesterol" over and over as fast as you can until you fall over.

Vitamins and Minerals

Vitamins and minerals are essential. They help other nutrients to work and can prevent certain diseases.

We need a Balance of Different Vitamins and Minerals

Vitamin A

1) We get most of our vitamin A from retinol, which is found in liver, butter, fish oils and eggs.
2) We can also make it from carotene, which is found in orange or yellow fruit and veg and margarine.
3) Vitamin A is needed for good eyesight (especially night vision) and growth and functions of tissues.

Vitamin B Complex

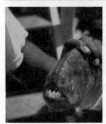

1) There are 8 different B vitamins (B1, B2, B3, B5, B6, B7, B9 and B12). Together they're known as Vitamin B Complex.
2) They're found in cereals, liver, kidney, peas, pulses, dairy produce, meat and fish.
3) B1, thiamin, helps the nervous system and the release of energy from carbohydrates. B2, riboflavin, helps with the release of energy and repair of tissues and B3, niacin, helps with the release of energy.
4) Folic acid is crucial for growth and important for women planning pregnancy, as low levels of folate at conception increase the risk of a baby having spina bifida.

Vitamin C (also known as Ascorbic Acid)

1) Vitamin C is found in citrus fruits (limes, oranges etc.), green veg, peppers and potatoes.
2) It's good for protecting the body from infection and allergies, helps in the absorption of calcium and iron from food, keeps blood vessels healthy and helps heal wounds.

Vitamin D (also known as Calciferol)

1) Vitamin D is found in oily fish and eggs and is produced in the body when the skin is exposed to sunlight.
2) It's good because it helps the body absorb calcium.
3) A lack of it can lead to bone diseases like rickets and osteoporosis.

Calcium

1) It's found in milk, tofu, salmon, green leafy vegetables, hard water and white bread.
2) It's needed for strong bones and teeth and healthy nerves and muscles.
3) Growing children need calcium every day for strong bones and teeth. Lack of calcium in youth can lead to problems in later life (e.g. osteoporosis).

Iron

1) Iron is found in dark green vegetables (e.g. spinach) and meat (especially liver and kidney).
2) It's needed to form part of the haemoglobin which gives blood cells their red colour. Lack of iron causes a deficiency disease called anaemia.

Sodium Chloride (Salt)

1) Salt is found in most foods, and some people add it to food as well.
2) It's needed to regulate the water content in the body, but too much salt's bad for you — it can lead to high blood pressure and heart disease.

Phosphorus

1) Phosphorus is found in foods like meat, fish, dairy products, nuts, beans and cereals.
2) It's needed for healthy bones and teeth. A lack of phosphorus can lead to weak muscles and painful bones.

What a complex page...

Loads and loads of info. And just in case you were wondering, yes, you do need to learn it all.

Vitamins and Minerals

Most Vitamins and Minerals come from Fruit and Veg

In a normal healthy diet, fruit and vegetables give you:

- The majority of your vitamin C intake (about 90%)
- Dietary fibre
- Vitamins A and B
- Iron and calcium
- Not much fat (except avocados)
- Loads of water
- Small amounts of protein.

Fruit and veg also make meals taste better — they give colour, texture, flavour, decoration, etc. They can also make a refreshing finish to a meal (e.g. a fruit salad), as well as a quick and easy snack.

You have to be careful when preparing fruit and veg to make sure that the nutrients aren't lost — see p17.

EXAM TIP
Make sure you know what each vitamin and mineral are needed for, and be able to name a good source of each one.

Nutrients can be Added to Foods

1) Sometimes extra nutrients are added to food — this is called fortification. It improves the nutritional value of foods.

2) Vitamins, iron and calcium are often added:

> Margarine is fortified with vitamins A and D, and iron is often added to breakfast cereals. Milk and flour can be fortified with calcium.

3) Fortification is done for different reasons — sometimes it's to replace nutrients that are lost during processing or to add extra nutrients to make it healthier.

Practice Questions

1) What foods do we get vitamin A from? Why do we need it?

2) List four types of B vitamin. For each one, state why it's useful.

3) What's the main vitamin found in oranges and lemons? How does it keep us healthy?

4) How does the body get vitamin D? What happens if we don't get enough of it?

5) a) List five good dietary sources of calcium.
   b) Look at Manfred, the dashing chap on the left. Why do our bodies need plenty of calcium?

6) Why is iron good for us? Name two good dietary sources of it.

7) Why do we need salt in our diet?

8) Name three foods that contain phosphorus.

9) Name six nutrients found in fruit and vegetables.

10) What's it called when extra nutrients are added to food?

11) Give two reasons why extra nutrients might be added to food.

Cereals, Wheat and Flour

Eating grass should mainly be left to cows and sheep, but certain members of the grass family are grown as food for humans (the seeds, not the blades of grass) — these are called cereals.

Cereals are used for Everything, Everywhere

1) Cereals contain lots of carbohydrates and are often used for their starchy properties.

2) They can be prepared in a variety of ways and used as part of a basic diet.

3) Some of the main cereals used are wheat, oats, barley, rye, rice, maize and millet.

The Grain is Made Up of Three Important Parts

1) Bran — the outside coat of the wheat, which provides dietary fibre.

2) Germ — a very small part of the grain, but provides vitamins and oils.

3) Endosperm — this forms the main part of the grain (85%). It's the white starchy part of the grain and provides protein and carbohydrate.

Staple Foods are Often Made from Cereals

Cereals can be processed and made into various products, which form the staple diet for people in many countries:

1) Bread, cakes and biscuits across the Western world are largely made with flour from wheat.

2) Italians use durum wheat to make pasta and cornmeal from maize to make polenta.

3) South Americans use cornmeal from maize to make cornbread.

4) Oatmeal is traditionally used in Scotland to produce biscuits and cakes as well as porridge.

5) Bread made from rye is eaten by people in Northern Europe.

6) Rice flour made from rice is often used in cakes and in Thai food.

There's a bit about how to cook and prepare staple foods on p16.

Cereals can also be used as part of a meal, like couscous with vegetable stew, or rice with curry.

Flour can be Made from Most Cereals

1) Cereals can be ground to make flour by a process called milling. Wheat flour is usually used in the UK.

2) There are three main types of wheat flour:

- Wholemeal flour — contains all of the wheat grain.
- Brown flour — contains about 85% of the grain, but some of the bran and wheat germ have been removed.
- White flour — made up of about 75% of the grain. Most of the germ and bran have been removed.

3) Wholemeal flour is more nutritious because it contains more fibre (as the bran's not taken away).

I could murder some cornflakes — I'm a cereal killer...

I'll bet you didn't realise that flour could be strong. Still, I don't care what anyone says, I'd rather fight the world's strongest flour than a hungry sumo wrestler. Either way, there'd be a nice, soft landing.

Cereals, Wheat and Flour

Flour has Many Different Uses

'Strong' flour is used to make bread

When dough made from 'strong' flour is kneaded, a protein called gluten is formed — it makes the dough stretchy and elastic. This helps the bread to rise and stretch during making and baking (see p18-19).

Using wholemeal flour can produce a loaf with a denser, closer texture because less gluten is formed. This problem can be overcome by using a mixture of strong white and strong wholemeal flour.

'Soft' flour is used to make cakes

'Soft' flour is more suitable for cake-making because less gluten is formed when it's mixed, so it produces a cake with a soft tender crumb. Lovely.

Flour can be used to thicken mixtures

Flour's often used to make mixtures thicker — e.g. cornflour is used to thicken gravies and sauces.

Raising Agents make Dough Rise

Holes formed by carbon dioxide bubbles

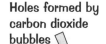

1) Raising agents are used in dough and cake mixtures to aerate them.
   They release bubbles of gas, which expand when heated to make the mixture rise.

2) Yeast is a biological raising agent used in bread dough — it's made up of microorganisms that cause fermentation, producing carbon dioxide. (Fermentation is when yeast breaks down the sugars in the dough, releasing carbon dioxide and alcohol.)

3) Baking powder and bicarbonate of soda are chemical raising agents.
   They break down when heated, producing carbon dioxide which makes cakes rise.

4) Self-raising flour has a controlled amount of raising agent added to it — it's often used in cakes.

Practice Questions

1) Name four different types of cereal.

2) Name the three different parts of a grain, and say which nutrients they are rich in.

3) Name a product that can be made from:
   a) durum wheat
   b) oatmeal

4) Name and briefly describe the three main types of wheat flour.

5) Why does wholemeal flour contain more fibre than white flour?

6) What's the name of the protein found in dough made from wheat flour?

7) What product would you make using:
   a) strong flour?
   b) soft flour?

8) Name three different raising agents and briefly describe how they work.

9) Bread can be used to make sandwiches, like this tasty-looking example.
   What is the best type of sandwich filling?

Target Groups

...Lifestyles and Religious Beliefs...

1) Your lifestyle can affect the foods you choose. <u>Athletes</u> and people with <u>active jobs</u> need foods that <u>provide energy</u>, slimmers and less active people need to eat <u>low-fat foods</u>.

2) <u>Convenience foods</u> are popular with people who lead <u>busy lives</u>. E.g. <u>cereal bars</u> can be eaten <u>on the go</u>, ready meals can be cooked <u>quickly</u>, and <u>fast food</u> is, well, fast.

3) Some people don't eat particular foods because of their <u>religion</u> e.g. Jewish people don't eat pork.

4) Cultural and religious festivals often have special products associated with them, e.g. <u>mince pies</u> at Christmas and <u>pancakes</u> on Shrove Tuesday.

...Advertising and Promotions...

1) <u>Trendy foods</u>, like <u>sushi</u>, can be popular. <u>Good advertising</u> and <u>celebrity endorsements</u> can help to boost the sales of particular products, brands or supermarkets (see next page).

2) <u>Special offers</u> on products attract customers who want to <u>save money</u>.

...Ethical Preferences...

See pages 36-37 for more on this.

1) Some people choose to buy <u>free-range</u> products because they know the animals are treated <u>ethically</u>.

2) Some people prefer to buy <u>organic foods</u> that are grown <u>naturally</u>.

3) <u>Fair trade products</u>, e.g. <u>bananas</u>, are popular with customers who want to make sure farmers get a <u>fair price</u> for their products.

EXAM TIP
You might have to explain how you'd <u>adapt</u> a product to make it suitable for a particular group.

4) Some people prefer to buy <u>British</u> or <u>local produce</u> or foods that are <u>in season</u> to support the <u>local economy</u> and to <u>reduce food miles</u> (see p42).

5) Some people <u>won't</u> eat fish that's becoming <u>endangered</u>, e.g. <u>bluefin tuna</u>.

6) Some people want to buy <u>sustainable</u> products (see p31).

...or just Give People What They Want

Not all target groups are to do with specific needs — <u>personal taste</u> can be just as important. People might like a product because:

"Go on, I'll let you try the steak first."

1) It <u>looks</u> or <u>tastes</u> good.
2) The <u>packaging</u> is appealing.
3) The food is terrifically <u>hot and spicy</u>.
4) Some people will <u>try anything</u> that's <u>new</u> and <u>exotic</u> — raccoon steak, anyone...

Other Factors also Affect People's Choice of Food

1) If you're on a budget you're more likely to buy <u>cheaper</u> products than expensive luxury products.

2) <u>Availability</u> — if your <u>local shops</u> don't sell octopus, you won't be able to buy octopus easily.

3) Your <u>storage</u> and <u>cooking facilities</u> will affect what you buy too, e.g. you wouldn't buy a microwave meal if you don't own a microwave, or a huge tub of ice cream if you don't have a freezer.

Practice Questions

1) What special requirements does a person with <u>coeliac</u> disease have?

2) How should a woman's diet change when she is <u>pregnant</u>?

3) Give two ways that <u>advertising</u> can affect people's food choices.

4) How might a person's <u>ethics</u> affect the products they buy?

Changing Trends

You might have thought that <u>trends</u> only affect things like <u>fashion</u>, but the <u>food</u> you eat is influenced too.

Globalisation has Affected the Food We Eat

1) Up until the middle of the 20th century, most food eaten in the UK was <u>grown</u> and <u>produced</u> here.
2) But as <u>trade</u> and <u>transport links</u> improved, it became common for food products to be grown, processed and sold <u>all over the world</u>. This is known as <u>globalisation</u>.
3) <u>Globalisation</u> means that <u>ingredients</u> from far-away countries are now more easily <u>available</u>, e.g. lemongrass and exotic fruits like pineapple and mango.
4) Good transport links also mean that people can <u>travel</u> more, and experience <u>different cultures</u> for themselves, as well as allowing people from other cultures to <u>come to the UK</u>. This increases our exposure to <u>multicultural foods</u>, so there's a greater <u>demand</u> for them.
5) It's now common for foods to be <u>grown</u> and <u>processed</u> in countries where labour is <u>cheaper</u>, before being sold <u>worldwide</u>. This makes the final product <u>cheaper to produce</u>.

Tastes Change According to Trends

<u>Manufacturers</u> need to <u>adapt</u> to new <u>trends</u> and <u>technologies</u> so that people keep buying their products.

1) After the Second World War, many people <u>emigrated</u> to the UK, bringing their own <u>cultures</u> and <u>foods</u> with them. This made <u>international</u> and <u>multicultural</u> foods (like curry) much more popular.
2) During the 1980s, <u>fridges</u>, <u>freezers</u> and <u>microwaves</u> became more common. Manufacturers quickly developed <u>new products</u> to take advantage of these <u>technologies</u> — e.g. Birds Eye produced <u>frozen foods</u>, and <u>microwavable meals</u> became popular.
3) As people's <u>lifestyles</u> got <u>busier</u>, the demand for quick-to-prepare foods increased. <u>Convenience foods</u> and <u>fast food</u> became popular — e.g. the first McDonald's opened in the UK in 1974.
4) From about 1990 onwards, people have become more concerned with <u>healthy eating</u>. People are also paying more attention to <u>where</u> products come from — so they may buy <u>local</u> (see p42), <u>fair trade</u> (see p37) or <u>organic foods</u> (see p38).

The Media Affect our Choices Too

The <u>media</u> influence what we buy, whether it's through clever <u>advertising</u> or what's reported in the <u>news</u>.

<u>Advertising</u> tries to encourage us to <u>buy products</u>, and can affect <u>food trends</u> too. <u>TV adverts</u> are usually <u>scheduled</u> to be on at times when their <u>target group</u> will be most likely to watch, e.g. children's snacks are often advertised in cartoon breaks (these can be high in salt and fat).

<u>Food scares</u> — where certain foods become linked to health problems, e.g. BSE and vCJD:

1) In the 1980s and 90s, lots of <u>beef cows</u> in the UK became infected with <u>BSE</u> (or mad-cow disease). Around the same time, some <u>people</u> were diagnosed with (and died from) a new human brain disease called <u>vCJD</u>. The two diseases are very <u>similar</u>, and it's thought that you could contract vCJD from eating <u>BSE-contaminated meat</u>.
2) When this news came out it caused a <u>food scare</u>, and beef sales <u>fell</u> dramatically — many people <u>stopped eating British beef</u>. Once the scare <u>died down</u> and <u>controls</u> had been put in place (to stop the disease getting in the food chain), people started eating British beef again.
3) Some people think scares are often <u>promoted</u> by the <u>media</u>, who provide <u>shock headlines</u> that make people buy the paper or watch the news.

I'd rather have a bowl of cardboard-flavoured muesli...

Some people think that advertising <u>unhealthy food</u> during <u>children's programmes</u> should be <u>banned</u> as it encourages children to eat foods that are <u>bad</u> for them, when they should be encouraged to eat healthily.

Changing Trends

Food Needs to be Produced Sustainably

Sustainability means providing enough resources without causing permanent damage to the environment or using up finite resources (ones that will run out).

RESOURCES ARE RUNNING OUT...

1) Some food resources are in short supply. For example, stocks of many popular fish are getting very low, e.g. cod, bluefin tuna.

2) The machinery needed to farm, process and transport food uses lots of energy. This energy usually comes from fossil fuels. These fuels are rapidly running out, and when they're burnt they release gases that add to global warming.

4) Product packaging uses up resources, e.g. trees for paper, oil for plastic, metal ores for cans.

5) Large areas of forest are often cleared to make way for intensive farming. Farming can lead to soil erosion, and the fertilizers used can damage the environment too.

6) Cattle and other animals produce gases that can cause global warming. The more cattle we raise to eat, the more gases are produced and the worse the effect on the environment.

...SO WE NEED TO USE RESOURCES IN A SUSTAINABLE WAY

1) Scarce food resources, e.g. cod stocks, need to be protected — cod can be protected by using a sustainable alternative like pollack.

2) Sustainable organic farming practices could be used, e.g. using manure instead of chemical fertilizers. (See p38 for more on organic foods).

3) Rather than using fossil fuels, electricity from renewable energy, e.g. solar power, could be used for processing food.

4) Less packaging could be used or packaging could be made from renewable resources. E.g. the wood pulp used to make cardboard often comes from plantations where enough trees are planted to replace those that are felled. Packaging can be reused and recycled (see p41), instead of thrown away in landfill sites.

A renewable resource is one that never runs out.

5) People could buy more locally produced or seasonal food that doesn't have to be transported as far.

6) Hedgerows can be planted around fields to help prevent soil erosion and provide habitats for animals.

7) Eating less meat would mean keeping less cattle, which would reduce the amount of harmful gases produced by animals.

Practice Questions

1) Explain what globalisation is, and how it affects the food we eat.

2) Explain how food manufacturers adapted to the inventions of freezers and microwaves.

3) Describe what is meant by a 'food scare'.

4) What does 'sustainability' mean?

5) Name two damaging effects of intensive farming.

6) What is a renewable resource?

7) A food processing company is concerned about environmental issues. They want to make some changes to how they make and package food. Suggest a renewable energy source that could be used to generate the electricity needed for processing food.

The 6Rs

The 6Rs crop up everywhere — they're important when you're thinking about sustainability or diet and nutrition. Learn them well and have them at the back of your mind whenever you're designing a product.

You Need to Know the 6Rs

> The 6Rs are: Recycle, Reuse, Reduce, Refuse, Rethink and Repair.

Using the 6Rs can help reduce the environmental impact of your lifestyle, as well as making it healthier.

They Can Help You Design a Sustainable Product

RECYCLE

1) Recycling means we reuse old resources instead of using up new ones.

2) Packaging can often be recycled — steel/aluminium, plastic, glass, card and paper are all recyclable. Some products have packaging made from recycled materials — e.g. a cereal box could be made from recycled cardboard.

3) Some types of packaging are biodegradable (they naturally rot in the environment) — so they won't add to landfill.

4) Some food waste (often veg scraps) can be composted.

> Although it saves resources, recycling sometimes takes more energy than making new products. It can also be expensive.

REUSE

1) Old products (or parts of them) can be used again for the same or a different purpose, e.g. glass or plastic bottles and containers can be reused at home. This stops more resources being used up.

2) Manufacturers can reuse leftover food, e.g. when sugar is made, the sugar beet waste can be used to feed pigs.

3) You can reuse leftovers at home too — e.g. you can use stale bread to make bread-and-butter pudding or bread crumbs.

REFUSE

1) Refuse to use packaging or ingredients that are unsustainable (see p31) — find alternatives.

2) Refuse to buy products with excess packaging.

REDUCE

1) Reduce the amount of resources you use when you make your product — like energy, ingredients, materials, chemicals (e.g. pesticides) and packaging.

2) Think about ways to reduce the energy used to cook or transport your product, e.g. changing the shape of packaging so lots can be transported together.

3) You can reduce waste by recycling and reusing things. Avoiding buying too much food helps you cut down on waste as well.

REPAIR

1) Lots of large, expensive equipment is used in food production. It should be kept in good condition and repaired when it breaks down so resources aren't used up making more.

2) Try and repair your home equipment before buying more. You can buy replacement parts for some things.

RETHINK

Don't get bogged down by traditional ideas — rethink how old products could be made in sustainable ways. E.g. reducing the packaging around an Easter egg.

Recycle, reduce, revise...

These pages are really really important — at least one of the 6Rs is bound to crop up in your exam. Learn them all, and make sure you can relate them to your diet, as well as sustainability...

The 6Rs

Four of the 6Rs Apply to Nutrition as well

Refuse, rethink, repair and reduce can help you improve your health — or the nutritional value of a product you're designing. Here's how:

REFUSE

Refuse to eat unhealthy products — products don't need to be high in fat, salt or sugar to taste nice.

RETHINK

1) Rethink how products could be made with lower fat, salt and sugar but still taste great.

2) Re-market 'healthy' products so they're more appealing.

EXAM TIP

The 6Rs crop up everywhere — make sure you can use them in relation to sustainability and nutrition.

REPAIR

Don't just think about low fat, sugar and salt. Think about how other nutrients help to repair and maintain a healthy body. Use these in your product, e.g. added vitamin C or folic acid.

REDUCE

1) You can reduce the amount of sugar, salt and fat you use — both in your diet and in your product.

2) Reducing the amount of processed foods you buy will help you do this.

Practice Questions

1) What are the 6Rs?

2) Name three materials used for packaging that can be recycled.

3) What are 'biodegradable materials'? Why are they better for the environment?

4) Give an example of how leftover food can be reused:
   a) at home
   b) in the food industry

5) Give an example of a food resource that isn't sustainable, and an example of what you could use as an alternative.

6) Jessica is looking at the packaging of different breakfast cereals. She finds one that has a lot of packaging that isn't really needed. Which of the 6Rs should she think about as she chooses her cereal?

7) Which four of the 6Rs relate to diet and nutrition?

8) What nutrients should you try to reduce in your diet?

9) Name two vitamins that can be used to help repair the body.

Choosing Ingredients

In industry, manufacturers don't always make their products from scratch...

Standard Food Components are Ready-Made Parts

1) Manufacturers can <u>buy in food parts</u> that have <u>already been made</u> by other manufacturers, e.g. pizza bases, fillings. These ingredients are called <u>standard food components</u>. They're <u>pre-manufactured components</u>.

2) Standard food components are <u>really useful</u> — they <u>cut out</u> a lot of <u>time</u> and <u>work</u>.

3) It's not just manufacturers — <u>catering businesses</u> and people cooking <u>at home</u> use standard food components too (see next page).

4) Standard components are <u>processed foods</u> — they've been <u>prepared</u>, <u>treated</u> or <u>altered</u> in some way. Highly processed foods often contain lots of <u>added sugar</u> and <u>salt</u> and can be <u>bad for your health</u>. Not all processed foods are bad for you though — things like <u>milk</u> and <u>fruit juice</u> are processed but are still <u>good</u> for you.

Using Standard Food Components has Advantages...

1) It <u>saves time</u> — you <u>don't</u> have to bother <u>preparing</u> the basic ingredients. This can improve your <u>quality of life</u>, as you get to spend more <u>time</u> with your <u>family</u>.

2) It <u>saves money</u> — manufacturers can often buy standard components <u>frozen</u>, <u>in bulk</u>, which is more <u>cost-effective</u> than buying fresh ingredients separately and making the components themselves.

3) <u>Less machinery</u> and <u>less specialist equipment</u> is needed, which also <u>saves money</u>.

4) <u>Fewer specialist skills</u> are needed by <u>staff</u> because the standard components are ready to use.

5) Food preparation is <u>safer and more hygienic</u> — especially if <u>high-risk</u> products like chicken, eggs or soiled vegetables are <u>stored and prepared somewhere else</u>.

The product is always the same.

6) The product is more likely to be <u>consistent</u> — standard food components are <u>quality-controlled</u> so they all have the <u>same</u> flavour, texture, weight, shape, colour, etc.

...and Disadvantages

The production line can be held up.

1) You <u>can't pick and choose</u> exactly what you want, e.g. you can't get the ready-made pastry made a tiny bit sweeter.

2) It's <u>not always reliable</u> — <u>late deliveries</u> from the supplier will hold up the production line.

3) The product <u>may not be as tasty</u> as one made with fresh ingredients.

4) <u>Extra space</u> might be needed to <u>store</u> the standard food components if you've bought them in bulk.

5) There may be <u>extra packaging</u> and <u>transport</u> involved, so it might be <u>bad for the environment</u>.

Broccoli — the standard food component used by all mums...

If you can stop drooling over cake for long enough to learn this, you'll see standard food components are dead useful. Your basic ingredients come ready-made — ace. If only exams came ready-answered.

Choosing Ingredients

Here are Some Examples of Standard Components

Pastry, Pizza Bases and Cake Mixes

Standard food components include things like <u>pizza bases</u>, <u>chilled and frozen pastry</u>, <u>cake mixes</u> and <u>bread mixes</u>. It's <u>much quicker</u> to start off with a ready-made component than to make it yourself — then you can <u>adapt</u> it as you need, e.g. you can put your own fillings into pies but start off with ready-made <u>pastry</u>.

EXAM TIP
You could get marks just for <u>naming</u> some standard components that might be used to make a product.

Fillings and Sauces

<u>Ready-made fillings</u> and <u>sauces</u> save you the bother of having to prepare all the separate ingredients. They also have a <u>longer shelf-life</u> than fresh products and can be <u>used at any time of year</u>, not just when the fresh products are in season. For example, you could make a <u>blackberry pie</u> in <u>January</u> if you used pie filling.

Icing and Marzipan

<u>Ready-to-roll icing</u> and <u>marzipan</u> are easy ways to <u>decorate</u> products without having to prepare everything yourself. For example, a cake business might order in ready-made <u>marzipan</u> in various colours, but <u>cut and shape it themselves</u> to make their decorations.

Using icing to decorate a cake is an example of a <u>finishing technique</u>.

It's Important to Reuse Leftover Ingredients

When you're choosing ingredients you should also think about the <u>environment</u> and <u>sustainability</u>, and remember your Rs (see p32):

1) <u>REUSE</u> — some products can be made from the <u>leftover ingredients</u> in your own kitchen, e.g. use chicken bones and vegetable scraps, like broccoli stalks, to make <u>stock</u>. Manufacturers can also use wonky or odd shaped vegetables that can't be sold in supermarkets (because they don't look as pretty) in things like <u>soups</u> — this means they aren't <u>wasted</u>.

2) <u>REDUCE</u> — reusing leftovers means you <u>reduce</u> the amount of <u>waste</u> you produce.

3) <u>RECYCLE</u> — any food that <u>can't</u> be reused (e.g. mouldy food or peelings) can be <u>recycled</u> by <u>composting</u>.

Practice Questions

1) Give two advantages and two disadvantages of using <u>standard components</u>.

2) Give three examples of standard components.

3) Name two ways you could use <u>leftover foods</u> to make a new food product.

Morals and Ethics

You might not think <u>morals</u> and <u>ethics</u> have much to do with Food Technology, but there's lots to consider — from how <u>animals</u> are treated to <u>working conditions</u> for people in <u>developing countries</u>.

Factory Farmed Animals Don't have Much Space

1) <u>Factory farmed</u> (or <u>battery farmed</u> or <u>intensively reared</u>) animals don't have <u>much room</u> to move.

2) They're kept <u>inside</u> in <u>warm sheds</u>, so they don't <u>waste much energy</u> moving or keeping themselves warm. That means that more of their energy goes into <u>producing meat</u> or <u>eggs</u> for food — this <u>maximises</u> food production.

3) Animals are sometimes given things like <u>growth hormones</u> or are <u>force-fed</u> to speed up their growth — making it even <u>quicker</u> and <u>cheaper</u> to produce meat.

4) Factory farmed food is generally <u>cheaper</u> than free-range (see below) — it's a more <u>efficient</u> way of farming, though it isn't as <u>ethical</u>.

5) People are becoming more <u>concerned</u> that intensively reared animals <u>don't</u> live very nice lives — they're more likely to suffer from <u>nasty diseases</u>, they can't <u>behave naturally</u> and they don't tend to <u>live as long</u>.

6) Generally, meat from factory farmed animals doesn't <u>taste as nice</u> as meat from free-range animals.

7) Battery farms are now <u>improving standards</u> to try to find a <u>compromise</u> between producing <u>large quantities</u> of <u>cheap food</u> and keeping the animals in <u>good conditions</u>.

Free-Range Animals have More Space

How animals that are kept for food are <u>cared for</u> is becoming more of a worry for many consumers. This has led to an increase in the number of people buying <u>free-range</u> food.

1) <u>Free-range food</u> (e.g. eggs) comes from animals that have <u>more space</u> to live than <u>factory farmed</u> animals — they're often <u>free to roam</u>.

2) Free-range animals have <u>different amounts</u> of room depending on the <u>brand</u> you buy, but they <u>all</u> have space to move and usually have <u>nicer lives</u> — they have a <u>higher standard of welfare</u>. <u>Free-range chickens</u> produce free-range eggs — they're allowed to <u>move around</u> more so they can <u>behave more naturally</u>.

Picture of happy, free-to-roam hens

3) <u>Less food</u> can be produced by rearing animals in free-range conditions — they take longer to grow, so the products are <u>more expensive</u> and might be beyond some people's budget.

4) Because many people are keen to buy ethical products, <u>companies</u> make it really clear that they use free-range products — they'll often make a <u>big deal</u> of it on their <u>packaging</u>.

> When you're <u>choosing</u> ingredients for products, you need to think about how important <u>morals</u> and <u>ethics</u> are to the people you're aiming at — will they value animal welfare above cost? This may affect choices like whether the ingredients you use are <u>free-range</u>.

The free-range radishes led long, happy lives...

More <u>ethical</u> products are generally more <u>expensive</u> — make sure you know the <u>reasons</u> why. In the end, the choice comes down to individual consumers, but you need to know all about the <u>moral issues</u>.

Morals and Ethics

Fair Trade Means Growers get a Fair Price

1) Growing and producing food can have social benefits, e.g. bringing new jobs to an area.

2) But companies also have a responsibility to make sure no one's health or way of life is harmed by making the products.

3) The fair trade movement tries to make sure that workers and farmers in developing countries are paid fairly and have good working conditions. There's a minimum price for fair trade produce, so it's usually more expensive (i.e. if the market value of a product drops, fair trade farmers aren't affected).

4) Through fair trade, workers can invest in their communities, e.g. to build schools or health centres.

5) The only downside to the scheme is that fair trade producers often produce a lot because of the good prices — and they sometimes produce too much. This can make world prices fall and cause producers who aren't in a fair trade scheme to lose out.

> **Fair Trade Certification**
>
> The FAIRTRADE Mark is used on products that meet international Fair trade standards, e.g. bananas, cocoa. It's the consumer's guarantee that producers have been paid an agreed and stable price which covers the cost of sustainable production.

The ETI is the Ethical Trading Initiative

Ethical trade is similar to fair trade. The Ethical Trade Initiative (ETI) helps workers get fair wages and good working conditions.

1) The ETI are involved in all areas and types of business — they work with traders, suppliers, workers, unions and charities in different industries (e.g. clothing, food and electrical).

2) They also try to ensure that workers are paid fair wages, don't have to work really long hours, are protected by health and safety laws and are allowed to join unions.

3) The ETI also works to raise awareness of workers' conditions, by making people more aware of the exploitation that can go on to make cheap products.

Once people are aware of these issues, they can make a moral choice to buy goods that are made fairly and ethically.

Practice Questions

1) How does factory farming maximise food production?

2) Why are factory farmed animals sometimes given growth hormones?

3) What are free-range products?

4) Why is free-range food often more expensive?

5) a) What is the fair trade movement?
   b) Give one advantage and one disadvantage of fair trade.

6) How does fair trade help communities?

7) a) What does ETI stand for?
   b) What does it do?

8) Why did the free-range chicken cross the road?

Section Three — Marketing and Packaging

Organic and GM Foods

People today are very concerned about <u>how</u> their food is <u>produced</u>, and what <u>effect</u> it has on the <u>environment</u>. <u>Organic foods</u> are very popular, while lots of people are wary of <u>GM foods</u>.

Pesticides can be Harmful to the Environment

1) <u>Pesticides</u> are <u>chemicals</u> and other substances used to <u>control pests</u> — <u>farmers</u> use them to <u>protect</u> their crops from <u>insects</u>, <u>weeds</u> and <u>fungi</u>.

2) However, pesticides can <u>harm wildlife</u> and damage the <u>environment</u>, e.g. by <u>polluting rivers</u>. Some of the chemicals can be harmful to <u>people</u> too.

3) Some farmers are trying to use <u>fewer chemical pesticides</u> and find <u>alternative methods</u> to control pests. These include things like:

- Introducing a pest's <u>natural predators</u> (e.g. ladybirds eat aphids).
- <u>Crop rotation</u> to prevent pests building up in the soil.
- <u>Biological pesticides</u> (e.g. certain fungi).
- Spraying crops with <u>hot water</u> instead of pesticides.

4) These alternatives are generally <u>better</u> for the environment, but can be <u>more expensive</u> and <u>less effective</u> than using chemical pesticides.

Organic Food Production Doesn't Use Pesticides

Organic food is <u>grown naturally</u>, but this makes it more <u>expensive</u> to produce.

1) Organic crops are grown <u>without</u> using <u>artificial chemicals</u> (like <u>pesticides</u> and <u>fertilizers</u>). Other techniques like <u>weeding</u> and using <u>manure</u> are used instead.

2) This means that more crops can be lost as artificial chemicals aren't used to <u>protect</u> them from pests.

3) Organic food <u>doesn't</u> usually contain any <u>GM ingredients</u> (see page 39).

4) Organic <u>meat</u> production has really high <u>animal welfare standards</u> and the animals aren't given <u>growth hormones</u>. That means that they take longer to grow, so the meat is more expensive.

Sally was the President of the Animal Welfare Union

Organic food can be both <u>good</u> and <u>bad</u> for the environment:

ADVANTAGES

- It <u>reduces</u> the amount of <u>chemical pesticides</u> going onto the land, so it's <u>less harmful</u> to the <u>environment</u>.
- It doesn't use <u>non-renewable resources</u> to make foods, so it's more <u>sustainable</u>.

Surprise, surprise — it helps if you remember the 6Rs (see page 32).

DISADVANTAGES

- Organic farming tends to produce a <u>lower yield</u> (less food from the same area of land).
- It's usually <u>more expensive</u>.

Altering genes — easy, just turn up the trouser legs...

Make sure you know about <u>organic</u> foods — including their <u>pros</u> and <u>cons</u>. You should be able to understand the <u>advantages</u> and <u>disadvantages</u> of using <u>Genetically Modified</u> products as well.

Organic and GM Foods

Genetically Modified Foods have Altered Genes

1) A genetically modified (GM) food is one that's had its genes altered to give it useful characteristics. GM plants are produced by inserting a desirable gene from another plant, an animal or a bacteria into the plant you want to improve. You plant modified seeds and up comes your GM crop.

2) For example, you can get GM maize that's pest-resistant. The farmer gets a bigger yield of maize because less of the crop is eaten or damaged by pests.

GM foods have advantages...

1) Crops can be made to grow quicker.
2) Producers can get higher yields of crops for the same amount of seed and fertiliser.
3) This makes food cheaper to produce so it's also cheaper for the consumer to buy.
4) Crops can be altered to have a longer shelf life — so less food is wasted.
5) Crops can be made to ripen earlier than normal, so fresh foods can be available for consumers earlier in the year.

...and disadvantages

1) GM foods haven't been around for long — so their long-term health effects aren't known.
2) There are concerns that modified genes could get out into the wider environment and cause problems, e.g. the weedkiller resistance gene could be transferred to a weed, making it a 'superweed'.
3) GM producers can't sell their food everywhere — the European Union (EU) restricts the import of some GM foods.

Consumers and the EU have Safety Concerns

Some people believe that we shouldn't mess about with genes because it's not natural.

To help consumers make an informed choice, the European Union (EU) has rules:

1) All GM foods must undergo strict safety assessments and they can only be sold if they're found to have no health risks.
2) All foods that are GM or contain more than 1% GM ingredients must be clearly labelled.

Practice Questions

1) What's a pesticide and what's it used for?
2) Name two negative effects of using chemical pesticides.
3) Give three alternative methods to using chemical pesticides.
4) What is an organic food?
5) Why is organic food generally more expensive?
6) What does GM stand for?
7) Give two advantages and two disadvantages of using GM foods.
8) Why do some people object to GM products?

Packaging and the Environment

Packaging is pretty useful — you wouldn't want to buy your food and then have it all <u>slopping about</u> and mixing together in your shopping bags... Even better, some packaging can stop food <u>going off</u>.

Packaging Contains, Protects and Preserves Food

Most food products are <u>packaged</u> before they're sold:

1) To <u>contain</u> the product neatly.
2) To <u>protect</u> it from being <u>damaged</u> while it's being transported, displayed and stored.
3) To <u>preserve</u> the food and <u>extend</u> its <u>shelf life</u> — otherwise it's more likely to be wasted.
4) To <u>avoid contamination</u>, e.g. from flies, vermin or people touching the food.
5) To <u>identify</u> what the product is and to give customers useful information.

There are <u>laws</u> about food packaging:

1) It can't be <u>hazardous</u> to human health.
2) It can't cause food to <u>deteriorate</u> (go off).
3) It can't cause an <u>unacceptable change</u> in a product's <u>quality</u>.

Different Types of Material are Used for Packaging

Various materials are used in different <u>shapes</u> and <u>thicknesses</u> to make packaging for different products.

GLASS, e.g. bottles, jars

- It's a <u>strong</u>, <u>rigid</u> material.
- It's <u>transparent</u> — customers can see what they're buying.
- It's <u>resistant</u> to high temperatures.
- It can be <u>reused</u> and is easy and cheap to <u>recycle</u>.

BUT...
- It's pretty <u>heavy</u>.   • Glass <u>breaks easily</u>.

PLASTIC, e.g. bottles, trays

- You can get <u>rigid</u> plastics and <u>flexible</u> ones.
- It can be <u>transparent</u> or <u>coloured</u>.
- Many types are <u>microwavable</u> — food can be heated in the packaging.
- It's <u>lightweight</u>.
- It can be <u>printed on</u>.

BUT...
- Most types <u>don't biodegrade</u>.
- Some plastic <u>can't</u> be recycled.

CARD and PAPERBOARD, e.g. boxes, packets

- Usually <u>biodegradable</u>.
- <u>Fairly strong</u>.
- <u>Lightweight</u> and <u>flexible</u>.
- Easy to <u>print on</u>.
- <u>Waterproof</u> if laminated.
- Easy and cheap to <u>recycle</u>.

BUT... You <u>can't see</u> the contents, and it's not very rigid, so the product may get <u>squashed</u>.

METALS (aluminium, tin), e.g. cans (see p57), foil

- Most metals are <u>strong</u> and some are fairly <u>light</u> e.g. aluminium.
- They're <u>resistant</u> to high temperatures.
- Aluminium is <u>cheaper</u> to <u>recycle</u> than to extract from the ground.

BUT... • Metals can <u>react</u> with some foods.
- You <u>can't see</u> the contents.

My paper milk bottle was a disaster...

Make sure you know why foods are packaged, and the different types of materials they can be packed in (including some pros and cons). Learn the environmental impacts too — and how to reduce them.

Packaging and the Environment

Packaging can be Bad for the Environment

1) <u>Manufacturing</u> packaging uses a lot of <u>energy</u> and <u>resources</u> — some of which are <u>non-renewable</u> (e.g. oil products are used to make plastic containers).

2) Most products need to be packaged to stop the food from getting <u>damaged</u> and <u>wasted</u>.

3) Some products have <u>excess packaging</u> just to make them look more attractive on the shelf — e.g. products that are shrink-wrapped <u>within</u> a box or other container.

4) Packaging often gets used <u>once</u>, <u>thrown away</u> and then just takes up space in Britain's already huge <u>landfill sites</u>. Not only is this a waste of the materials, but some packaging, like <u>plastics</u>, take a long time to <u>biodegrade</u>, and could <u>take up space</u> in a landfill site for years.

5) Packaging also adds to the <u>weight</u> of a product, so <u>transporting</u> it (see p42) uses more energy. This uses up more <u>fossil fuels</u> and produces more <u>greenhouse gases</u>, which add to <u>global warming</u>.

You can Reduce the Environmental Impact

There are lots of ways to <u>reduce</u> the <u>environmental impact</u> of packaging:

1) You can <u>recycle</u> tins, plastic, glass, card and paper — look out for this symbol:

2) You can buy products with <u>little</u> or <u>no packaging</u> — or <u>refuse</u> to buy products with <u>excess packaging</u>. This is even <u>better</u> than recycling it. Also, products with less packaging are often <u>cheaper</u>, as manufacturers don't have to spend money on it.

3) You can choose products with <u>biodegradable packaging</u>.

4) You can choose products with packaging <u>made</u> from <u>recycled materials</u> — they may not look as <u>pretty</u>, but they're <u>better</u> for the <u>environment</u>.

5) You can carry your food in <u>reusable shopping bags</u> — this reduces the need for <u>plastic bags</u>, which end up in <u>landfill</u>.

In 1997, the Government made a set of <u>rules</u> for all businesses that manufacture, fill or sell packaging. The point was to:

> 1) Increase the amount of packaging that can be <u>recycled</u>.
> 2) <u>Reduce</u> the amount of packaging in total.

EXAM TIP
If you get a question on packaging in your exam, make sure you think about the 6Rs (see p32).

Practice Questions

1) Give three reasons why food is <u>packaged</u>.

2) State three things food packaging is <u>not</u> allowed to do.

3) Simon is deciding which <u>material</u> to use for his packaging.
   a) Give two advantages and two disadvantages of using <u>glass</u>.
   b) Give two advantages and two disadvantages of using <u>metals</u>.

Ha ha ha

4) Charlotte is making a <u>microwavable meal</u> that can be cooked in its packaging. What type of <u>material</u> should she use for her packaging?

5) Give three ways that packaging can be <u>bad</u> for the environment.

6) Give two ways that you can <u>reduce</u> the <u>environmental impact</u> of packaging.

7) Martyn laughs in the face of packaging, but some manufacturers don't. Name two things <u>manufacturers</u> have to do to <u>reduce</u> their <u>environmental impact</u>.

Section Three — Marketing and Packaging

Transport and Labelling

Your food doesn't just magically appear in the supermarket — some of it's travelled thousands of miles.

Some Food comes from Different Countries

TRANSPORTING FOOD HARMS THE ENVIRONMENT...

1) Some food is transported a long way to be sold, e.g. some green beans you buy in the UK have come from Kenya. This can be expensive, and it's also bad for the environment. Planes, ships and trucks all burn scarce fossil fuels and release carbon dioxide into the atmosphere, contributing to global warming.

2) But consumers want food to be available all year round, not just when it's in season here. So shops and manufacturers buy food from abroad when it's out of season at home, e.g. asparagus has a very short season here. Also, some things just can't be grown here, like bananas.

3) Transport costs (and environmental impact) can be kept down by using packaging that stacks well — to fit as much as possible on each lorry.

EXAM TIP
With questions on this kind of stuff, don't write things like "because it's bad for the environment" — explain why it's bad.

Food miles is the distance food travels from where it's produced to where it's sold.

A greener way to transport bananas.

...SO LOCAL AND SEASONAL FOOD IS BEST

1) To reduce food miles, some people try to only buy local products — farmers' markets are a good source of local products.

2) So, if you're developing a fruit tart, consider whether the fruits you intend to use are available locally and whether they're in season.

You Can Measure Environmental Impact

Your Carbon Footprint measures the impact your lifestyle has on the environment — in terms of the amount of greenhouse gases produced (especially carbon dioxide). Burning fossil fuels for heat, electricity, transport etc. increases your carbon footprint.
Foods have a carbon footprint too — and the further a product has to travel, the larger its carbon footprint.

A product's Life-Cycle Analysis works out the environmental impact of a product at every stage of its life. It goes from sourcing the materials to disposing of the waste produced (and every step on the way, e.g. transport).

Your Eco Footprint is a bit like a carbon footprint, but it measures the way you use the planet's natural resources and how much waste you produce, and balances it against how well the Earth can produce new resources and absorb your waste.

Fridge to table — 0.05 miles...

There are loads of ways to reduce the impact of food transportation on the environment — so make sure you know lots of examples. Learn all the stuff on labelling too — like what must go on a label.

Transport and Labelling

Labels Must Tell You Certain Information by Law

The law says that the label on pre-packed food has to tell you all this stuff:

California Orange Juice*

* Made in the UK

1) The name of the product and what it is (if the name doesn't make it obvious).

2) The weight or volume of the product.

3) How to store the product and a use by date or a best before date.

4) The name and address of the manufacturer.

5) The country it comes from if the purchaser might be confused. E.g. if there's a Jamaican flag on the label but the product was made in the UK, it must say 'Made in the UK'.

6) Cooking instructions, if the product needs cooking. E.g. the required temperature and cooking time.

7) A list of ingredients, including any additives and genetically modified ingredients (see p39). This means people with allergies or special dietary needs can check if the product is OK for them. They're listed in descending order of weight — so the main ingredients are listed first.

Nutritional Information is Needed to Back up Claims

1) Lots of products list nutritional information but they don't have to by law...

2) ...UNLESS they make a special nutritional claim, such as 'low-fat' or 'high in fibre'.

3) Nutritional information is usually shown in a table listing energy content, protein, carbohydrate, etc.

4) Claims such as 'low-fat' can only be made if the nutritional information backs this up.

NUTRITIONAL INFORMATION		
	per 100g	per 55g serving
Energy	2180kJ/525 kcal	1199kJ/289 kcal
Protein	6.5g	3.6g
Carbohydrate	50.0g	27.5g
of which sugars	2.0g	1.1g
Fat	33.0g	18.2g
of which saturates	15.0g	8.3g
Sodium	0.7g	0.4g
Fibre	4.0g	2.2g

1 kcal is 1 calorie.

Other information doesn't have to be there but manufacturers try to make their label useful to consumers.

- Symbols are used to show that food is suitable for a particular diet, e.g. food suitable for vegetarians is often indicated with a green V.

- Possible allergy problems can be highlighted, e.g. 'may contain traces of nuts'.

- Traffic-light labelling on a product shows how healthy it is at a glance. Red, orange and green colours show whether a product has high, medium or low amounts of saturated fat, salt and sugar.

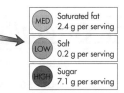

MED — Saturated fat 2.4 g per serving
LOW — Salt 0.2 g per serving
HIGH — Sugar 7.1 g per serving

Practice Questions

1) Explain how transporting food harms the environment.

2) a) What are food miles?
   b) Give one way of reducing food miles when you shop.

3) Describe what a Carbon Footprint is.

4) Describe what an Eco Footprint is.

5) Name five things that must appear on a food label.

6) When do products have to show nutritional information?

7) Name three other things that might be shown on a food's packaging.

Design and Research

The process of <u>designing</u> and <u>making</u> something is called '<u>the design process</u>' (gosh). The whole process can take a while — so, like many pineapples, it's usually broken down into smaller <u>chunks</u>.

The Design Process is Similar in Industry and School

The things you'll have to do for your <u>project</u> and for the <u>design question</u> in the exam are pretty similar to what happens in <u>industry</u>. Remember:

- The best products are those that address a <u>real need</u>.
- That's why companies spend so much <u>time</u> and <u>money</u> on <u>consumer research</u>. The more people there are who would actually <u>use</u> a product, the more chance the product has of being a <u>roaring success</u>.

You need to think about food trends (see p30) and identify potential gaps in the market.

The rest of this section describes a <u>typical design process</u> — it shows the sort of thing that happens in <u>industry</u> every day. You need to understand the <u>overall process</u>.

Decide Who to Aim Your Product At

Even the very best products aren't everyone's cup of tea — some people <u>like</u> them and some <u>don't</u>.

Your <u>target group</u> is the group of people you want to sell your product to. You should ask <u>that group of people</u> what they want the product to be like.

See pages 28-29 for more info on target groups.

You can group people by features like <u>age</u>, <u>gender</u>, <u>job</u>, <u>hobbies</u>, <u>lifestyle</u>, <u>income</u> or anything else — it'll probably be a combination of a few of these things.

For example... if you're trying to sell an <u>organic reduced-fat meat substitute</u>, you may decide to target it at <u>middle-aged vegetarians</u> who are trying to <u>lose weight</u>.

It Starts With a Design Brief

The <u>design brief</u> explains <u>why</u> there's a need for a new product. It usually includes:

1) an <u>outline</u> of the <u>context</u> (background) and <u>who</u> the product's aimed at,
2) what <u>kind</u> of product is needed,
3) how the product will be <u>used</u>.

The design brief is <u>short</u> and to-the-point — it's basically a <u>starting point</u> for the development of the product.

Think Carefully About What You Want to Find Out

Once you've decided on your target group, you need to decide what to <u>ask</u> them. You could find out:

1) Some info about the <u>person</u>. (This could help you make sure they're within your <u>target group</u> or give you <u>extra info</u>.)
2) If they already <u>buy</u> the kind of product you're thinking of developing.
3) If they like a particular <u>flavour</u> or <u>colour</u>.
4) <u>When and where</u> they buy the product and where they <u>consume</u> it.
   (This could affect the <u>packaging</u> you use.)
5) If they'd <u>want</u> to buy <u>your version</u> of the product. (Explain the advantage of your product over existing brands — would that be enough to tempt them to buy your version?)
6) If there's something they <u>would like</u> from your product that existing brands <u>don't have</u>.

Triceratops flavoured crisps, now THAT'S what you need.

Design briefs — much more fun than design vests and socks...

Can you believe all this <u>effort</u> goes into a humble custard tart? Mind you, if you don't put this much thought into designing your product, you probably won't get very good marks, so it's worth the effort.

Design and Research

Questionnaires are Forms for People to Fill In

When you write a questionnaire, you should include:

1) A <u>title</u> — for example it could be 'Questionnaire Researching Favourite Puddings'.

2) A <u>brief explanation</u> of the purpose of the questionnaire.

3) A <u>mixture of question types</u> and <u>not too many</u> questions, so people don't get bored and give up answering them.

Weirdo...

A quick way to assess the market and to see what other products are available is to use the <u>internet</u>. You can also check out the product reviews written by customers.

There are three basic types of question:

1) <u>Closed Questions</u> — these have a <u>limited number of possible answers</u>, e.g. <u>do you like puddings</u>? <u>Analysing</u> the results is easy for this type of question, e.g. by using <u>graphs</u> or <u>charts</u>, as it's easier to show a limited number of answers on a graph.

2) <u>Open Questions</u> — these have <u>no set answer</u>, e.g. <u>why is that your favourite pudding</u>? They give people a chance to provide <u>details</u> and <u>opinions</u>. This type of questioning is more <u>time-consuming</u> and it's <u>harder</u> to draw conclusions from the results, as there could be too many different answers to fit on a graph. But you could gain <u>valuable information</u>.

You could include <u>images</u> and ask people which product looks most <u>attractive</u>.

3) <u>Multiple choice questions</u> — these give a <u>choice</u> of answers. Sometimes the person answering can pick more than one.

Q4. What kind of puddings do you like?		
Chocolate puddings ☑	Ice cream ☐	Slug puddings ☑

Interviews are Face-to-Face Conversations

1) For interviews, you can <u>start off</u> by asking the same sort of questions as in questionnaires — but then take the opportunity to ask <u>follow-up</u> questions, based on the answers you get. E.g. if their favourite pudding is trifle, ask them <u>why</u> they like it.

"I can't STAND the smell of tuna..."

2) Interviews can give you more <u>detailed</u> information than questionnaires — you can have short <u>conversations</u> with people you're aiming to sell to. Just make sure you <u>stick to the point</u>.

3) Conversations mean your interviewees give <u>extra information</u> to explain their answers — this might give you more <u>ideas</u> for your product.

4) A problem with interviews is that it's sometimes more <u>difficult</u> to <u>analyse</u> the results than with questionnaires because you might have asked different people different follow-up questions.

Practice Questions

1) Why do companies think <u>consumer research</u> is so important?

2) What information does a <u>design brief</u> give? Why is it important?

3) a) What is a <u>target group</u>?
   b) What <u>features</u> can you use to describe a target group?
   c) List five sensible things you could <u>ask</u> a target group if you were making a new kind of <u>salad</u>.

4) Imagine you are researching opinions about a new <u>sandwich</u> product. Write one example of:
   a) a <u>closed</u> question   b) an <u>open</u> question   c) a <u>multiple choice</u> question

Analysis

Manufacturers don't often develop a <u>brand new</u> product — they usually <u>redesign</u> an existing one.
First, they do a <u>product analysis</u> — on their own or a competitor's product — to find ways to improve it.

Start With Disassembly and Packaging Analysis

<u>Disassembly</u> means taking a product apart and examining the bits. When you do this, take a <u>photo</u>
of the <u>packaging</u> and <u>food</u> before you start. And remember to <u>make notes</u>. Write about:

1) The <u>measurements</u> of the product — make a table
    showing the <u>weight</u> of each ingredient.
    E.g. if you're disassembling a cheese and tomato
    sandwich, weigh the cheese, tomato and bread.
    This will let you work out the <u>proportions</u> of each thing.

Bread	63 g
Cheese	32 g
Tomato	29 g

There's about twice as much bread as there is cheese.

There's about the same weight of tomato as cheese.

2) The <u>textures</u> and <u>colours</u> of the various parts of the product, e.g. "It has a flaky golden crust".
    (Describe the texture using words like dry, moist, crunchy, creamy, etc.)

3) How the product is <u>put together</u> and how you think it was made, e.g. "The cheese is added last".

4) How it <u>tastes</u>, <u>smells</u> and <u>looks</u>. Be specific, e.g. "It's very bitter", <u>not</u> "It's horrible".

5) Whether it's <u>fit</u> for its <u>intended user</u>, i.e. nutritional value, packaging etc.

6) Its <u>environmental impact</u>, as well as any <u>moral</u> and <u>cultural</u> issues (see Section 3).

The <u>packaging</u> is also useful — it shows you more detail about the product.

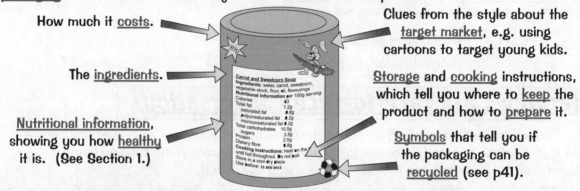

How much it <u>costs</u>.

The <u>ingredients</u>.

<u>Nutritional information</u>, showing you how <u>healthy</u> it is. (See Section 1.)

Clues from the style about the <u>target market</u>, e.g. using cartoons to target young kids.

<u>Storage</u> and <u>cooking</u> instructions, which tell you where to <u>keep</u> the product and how to <u>prepare</u> it.

<u>Symbols</u> that tell you if the packaging can be <u>recycled</u> (see p41).

Use the Info to Make Your Product Better

After you've analysed a product, decide its <u>faults</u> and find ways to make yours <u>better</u>. Think about:

1) The <u>quality</u>, <u>quantity</u> and <u>proportions</u> of the <u>ingredients</u>.

2) The <u>size</u>, <u>shape</u>, <u>weight</u>, <u>appearance</u>, <u>texture</u> and <u>flavour</u>.

3) The quality and effectiveness of the <u>packaging</u> and its impact on
    the <u>environment</u> — is your product <u>sustainable</u>? (See p31.)

4) The <u>price</u> — if you think it's too expensive for what it is,
    say why, by how much and how to make it cheaper.

5) The <u>nutritional value</u>.

"Brilliant! Sausage with eggs, I bet no one's ever thought of that before..."

Think about using local ingredients — see page 42.

When you <u>write out</u> how to make it better, be <u>clear and exact</u>. E.g. if you reckon the original looks a bit pale and unappealing, <u>don't</u> just say "make it look nicer" — say something like "make sure the cheese topping is golden-brown in colour".

Get me a drill — prepare to be disassembled, Mr Scone...

Ah, there's nothing like being critical. And there's loads to think about and try to <u>improve</u> — maybe the food could be cooked or stored differently, perhaps it should be aimed at a different target market...

Analysis

Use Sensory Analysis to Find Out What People Like

Sensory analysis is <u>tasting</u> samples of food and <u>rating</u> how good they are. Manufacturers ask <u>consumers</u> to do it, to find out what they think about new or existing products. This helps the manufacturer decide what characteristics their new product should have. <u>Rating</u> or <u>ranking</u> tests are commonly used:

Ranking Testing

<u>Ranking Test</u> Name: *Delia Quiff*	
Taste the samples and place them in order of preference	
Sample code	Order of Preference
SPE12	2nd
SPE14	1st

Rating Testing

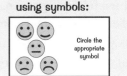

using symbols:
Circle the appropriate symbol

using numbers:
1 = Hate
2 = Dislike
3 = It's OK
4 = Like
5 = Love

In a <u>rating</u> test, you give products a score — in a <u>ranking</u> test, you put them in order of preference.

EXAM TIP
You might be asked what the difference between a ranking and a rating test is.

Do Your Sensory Analysis Properly

You need a <u>group of people</u> to be <u>testers</u> — ideally people from the <u>target group</u>.

1) Use a <u>quiet area</u> and give tasters <u>water</u> to sip to separate the tastes of different products.

2) Use <u>small amounts</u> of food and clean spoons. Don't let people put <u>used spoons</u> in the food.

3) Use <u>codes</u> or symbols for the products, to make sure the tasters aren't influenced by the name.

4) Make sure the tasters <u>understand</u> what they're meant to do.

Record Your Results to Show What You've Found Out

Star Profiles

Testers <u>rate</u> the main <u>characteristics</u> of a product on a <u>scale of 1-5</u>. Each <u>leg</u> of the diagram represents a <u>characteristic</u>. The marks are then joined up, showing which aspects people <u>like</u> and which they <u>don't</u> — e.g. in this example, the testers liked the smell and the taste, but not the colour.

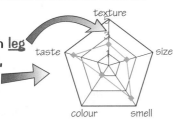

Q. What is your favourite type of pasta?

A:

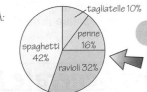

Charts

You can use <u>pie charts</u>, <u>bar charts</u>, etc. — they allow you to see <u>at-a-glance</u> what your results show — e.g. here, spaghetti is the most popular type of pasta.

Practice Questions

1) What does "<u>disassembly</u>" mean?

2) List three useful things you can find on the <u>packaging</u> of a food product.

3) Name five <u>faults</u> you might find in an existing product that you could improve on.

4) What's the point of <u>sensory analysis</u>? Name a common sensory analysis <u>test</u>.

5) The <u>star profile</u> on the right shows the results of some sensory analysis on a new sandwich product you've designed. Based on these results:
   a) What aspects about the sandwich would you try to <u>change</u>?
   b) What aspects would you <u>keep the same</u>?

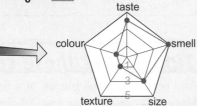

Design Specification

When you've done your research, you can sit back and put your feet up. Oh no sorry, nothing of the sort.

Do Research to Help With Your Design

The design brief helps you decide which products to analyse and what you need to research.
You should have loads of information from your research — you can use it to help with your design.

1) Summarise what you've found out — pick out the most important and useful findings, e.g. "Hedgehogs are a popular ingredient in breakfast cereals".

2) Explain what impact the research will have on your designs, e.g. "Hedgehogs will be a major ingredient".

3) Suggest ways forward from the research you've done, e.g. "One idea would be to add spines to the cereal".

You Need a List of Design Criteria

EXAM TIP
You normally get given a design specification in the exam, and have to design a product from it.

1) The conclusions from your research should show what kind of characteristics your product needs to have.

2) These requirements are your design criteria. A list of design criteria is called a design specification.

3) Each of the criteria in a design specification says one thing about what the product should be like, e.g.

> Design Specification for a New Pudding
> • it must have an attractive topping
> • It could be chocolate-flavoured
> • It must be big enough to feed 8 people

4) You don't have to be really exact at this point — that comes later (see page 52). Just a few words for each point is enough.

5) But you do need to show how the criteria are related to your research — e.g. it's fair enough to have "the omelette must be hexagonal" as one of your criteria, but only if your research analysis concludes that people want a hexagonal omelette — don't just make it up because it sounds interesting.

There are Tricks that can Help You Generate Ideas

1) Work from an existing product or recipe — but change some of its features or production methods so that it fits in with your design specification, e.g. the colour, size, ingredients, etc.

2) Think about the functionality of the product — how well it meets the needs of your target group. You also need to think about how well your idea meets the design brief and specification.

3) Think about how to get the aesthetics you want — how your product looks, smells and tastes like. How will you get the texture you want? What about the nutritional content?

4) It may help to do a spot of brainstorming... (see next page).

Time to get those creative juices flowing...

And now, drum roll please, it's time to get creative and doodle some weird and wonderful design ideas.
Hooray — about time too, I hear you shout. Well yes (but the other stuff was important you know).

Design Specification

Brainstorm to Produce Initial Ideas

Show your ideas clearly — they'll be worth a fair few marks in your exam.

1) First, think up <u>key words</u>, <u>questions</u> and <u>initial thoughts</u> about your product.

2) <u>Don't</u> be too <u>critical</u> at this stage — let your <u>imagination</u> run wild. Even if an idea sounds ridiculous, put it down anyway.

3) Be <u>creative</u> and get <u>as many ideas</u> as you can. Afterwards, decide which ones are <u>good</u> (and so are worth developing) and which ones are as <u>stupid</u> as a wooden blancmange.

4) Use <u>word association</u> (a type of brainstorming) — choose a product and write down any related words. E.g. <u>biscuits</u>, <u>mouse</u>, <u>straws</u>, <u>melt</u> and <u>smelly</u> are all associated with... <u>cheese</u>.

Research Summary:
- healthy products are popular
- bread is boring
- spicy is good

Design Specification:
- must be low in fat
- must appeal to young people
- must be multi-cultural

Key words:
- innovative
- tasty
- convenient
- spicy

Chip Butty with Quorn™

Low-fat Croissants

Mr Gobble's Exceedingly Spicy Crumpet Vindaloo

IDEAS FOR LOW-FAT BREAD PRODUCTS

Spicy Veg Patty Sandwich

Grilled Artichoke English Muffins

Questions:
- Can croissants be made low-fat?
- How long will Quorn™ keep?
- Will crumpets appeal to young people?

You need to Come up With a Range of Designs

Link the features to your design criteria.

1) Once you've sorted out the good ideas from the bad ones, <u>annotate</u> (i.e. add <u>notes</u> to) each good design idea to fully <u>explain</u> what it is and why it's good. You could mention features like:
   • materials needed • target group • cost • size • shape • advantages / disadvantages

2) You need to produce a <u>range</u> of different solutions — about 3 or 4 — that meet the design specification.

3) It's also important that you think you could actually <u>make</u> them — don't go overboard on exciting ideas that you could never produce for real.

Present Your Ideas Clearly

1) To <u>present</u> your ideas, it's usually best to keep it simple — a <u>freehand sketch</u> will do fine, as long as it's <u>clear</u>.

2) Once you've got a few possible designs, have a good <u>think</u> about them all, and decide which is the <u>best idea</u> — i.e. the one that most closely matches the design brief and design specification. This is the one you should <u>develop</u>.

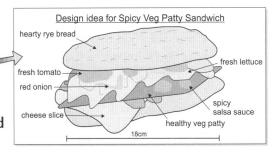

Design idea for Spicy Veg Patty Sandwich

hearty rye bread — fresh lettuce — fresh tomato — red onion — cheese slice — spicy salsa sauce — healthy veg patty — 18cm

Practice Questions

1) What is a <u>design specification</u>?

2) Read the research summary about desserts and make a short list of possible <u>design criteria</u> based on it:

3) Describe two ways you could <u>generate product ideas</u>.

4) a) What should you do <u>after</u> you've come up with plenty of ideas?
   b) Give one way you could <u>present</u> your ideas.
   c) How do you know which of your ideas is the best one to <u>develop</u>?

Most people prefer chocolate flavoured desserts to fruit flavoured ones. However, they are worried that these might not be healthy — the majority want the product to be low in calories, but still to taste very sweet and chocolatey. Texture is also important — runny desserts are less popular than more solid ones.

Development

So now it's time to give your product a try — yep, actually <u>make</u> it — and then make <u>improvements</u> to it.

You can Develop Your Design in Different Ways

Depending on the <u>type</u> of product that's being produced, there are a few ways you can develop it.

1) You could make some more detailed <u>sketches</u>. This might help you decide on some of the <u>smaller details</u> you hadn't thought about before, e.g. how the different toppings of a pizza would be arranged.

2) Do some <u>practical experimentation</u> with different aspects of the design. You could:

- change an <u>ingredient</u>, e.g. soft brown sugar instead of caster sugar
- change a <u>component</u>, e.g. pears instead of apples
- change the <u>equipment</u>, e.g. mix by machine instead of using a spoon
- change the <u>process</u>, e.g. add the cheese last, before baking.

"This time I'll try using a spoon to mix it instead of using my fingers."

Trying out different versions of your design is called <u>modelling</u> — and each different version is a <u>model</u>. *(See below for more on modelling.)*

3) Use your <u>target group's opinions</u> about developments to help you give them what they want.

Make Changes and Compare Models

1) After you've made the first real <u>model</u> of your design idea (called a <u>prototype</u>), you need to do some <u>tests</u> to check it's how you wanted it to be — this is called <u>evaluation</u>.

If your product is for <u>freezing and reheating</u>, you'll need to try doing that — and then evaluate the product <u>after reheating</u>.

2) These tests could cover <u>appearance</u>, <u>texture</u>, <u>taste</u>, <u>smell</u> and other things. Check it against all the criteria in the <u>design specification</u> too.

> It's dead important that your sensory analysis (see p47) and other tests are <u>thorough</u> and <u>rigorous</u> — you need to be <u>super-critical</u> of your model so that you can make the final product as good as possible.

3) You'll probably find there are some things in your initial model that <u>didn't work out</u> the way you'd hoped — maybe it <u>tasted great</u> but was really <u>expensive</u>, in which case you could try using some cheaper ingredients or making a smaller product.

The sponge cake was too greasy, so in the next model I'm going to try using butter instead of lard.

4) The evaluation of the <u>first</u> model might give you <u>ideas</u> about what <u>modifications</u> are worth a try. So make the changes and <u>try again</u>. Use a <u>digital camera</u> to record each model you make.

5) Put <u>each model</u> you make through the <u>same</u> tests. That way you can compare them <u>fairly</u> and see if you've actually improved things.

> Development is a vital part of the design process. Ideally you should <u>solve all the potential problems</u> with your design at this stage.

Dehydrated water — it's got to be a winner...

<u>Modelling</u> and <u>evaluation</u> go hand in hand. It's pointless baking a cake and eating it if you're not going to bother learning anything from it. Ah, well... maybe not actually. If it's a really big cake.

Development

Keep Going Until You Get it Just Right

You might have to modify quite a few aspects of your design. For example, you could try changing:

1) The <u>ingredients</u> you use (or what proportions you use or how you combine them).

2) The <u>shape</u> or <u>size</u> of the product — you could use try using a different shaped tin for a cake, say.

3) The <u>finish</u> — for example you could add a glaze (see p25), or grill something briefly to brown it on top.

> Changing <u>one thing</u> might mean you need to change <u>something else</u>.

For example, say you bake a cake in a wide, circular tin instead of a deep, loaf-shaped tin. The cake will now be <u>thinner</u> and could burn more easily... so you might have to alter the <u>cooking time</u> or <u>temperature</u>.

Here's a summary of how development works — <u>every time</u> you try something new:

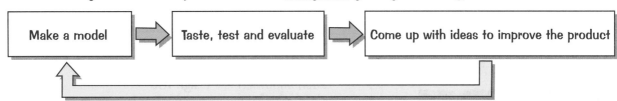

| Make a model | → | Taste, test and evaluate | → | Come up with ideas to improve the product |

Remember to note down what you're changing and why.

That shows you're doing things properly.

1) You might have to keep <u>changing</u> your product to make sure you meet the design specification. That's fine — the whole point of development is to find out what works and what doesn't.

2) But you <u>can't change</u> the <u>design specification</u> — because then you probably wouldn't be meeting the design brief any more.

3) In other words, you've got to make your product fit the design specification, not the other way round.

Part of your design brief might be to make your product <u>environmentally-friendly</u> — so you'd need to think about these kind of things:

1) Are your ingredients from a <u>local</u> source? (This helps to reduce pollution because they don't travel as far.)

2) Are your materials <u>sustainable</u>? (This means you're not using up natural resources until they run out.)

3) Can you reduce the amount of <u>waste</u> food and materials? (Think what you can reuse before throwing it away.)

4) How much <u>energy</u> is used to make your product? (Reduce energy used, or use renewable energy.)

See page 32 for more on environmental issues.

Practice Questions

1) This young man is doing a spot of <u>modelling</u>.
   What does <u>modelling</u> mean in Food Technology?

2) Imagine you are developing a new type of <u>sponge pudding</u> that has to be tasty but low in fat. You make the first version of the product. Unfortunately it <u>fails</u> your sensory analysis tests, so you try <u>changing the ingredients</u>. Suggest <u>two other changes</u> you could try.

3) Imagine you are making a new kind of low-cost <u>pizza</u>, but your first model's texture is too <u>dry</u>. Describe two ways you could try developing your product to <u>improve the texture</u>.

4) Why can't your <u>design specification</u> change during the development of a product?

Planning Production

Once you've developed your idea, you're ready to put together a <u>product specification</u>.
And it can't get much more exciting than writing your own specification points all about food... can it...

The Product Specification Describes the Product

1) The product specification expands on your chosen idea and says exactly <u>what the product is</u>, not just what it tries to do.

2) It <u>describes</u> what the product contains, how it looks and tastes and so on. It should have <u>exact</u> figures and measurements.

3) In your product specification, include <u>some</u> or <u>all</u> of the following:

   - how it will look
   - how it will taste
   - how it should be stored
   - size and weight
   - safety points
   - costs

4) Put your specification together using <u>bullet points</u> rather than wordy explanations.

- Each sandwich will weigh 180-200 grams.
- Manufacturing cost will be under 75p per unit.
- It will use brown bread.
- It will have a ham, cheese and mustard filling.
- The primary flavour will be cheese, with a spicy after-taste.

Use words like "will", "should" and "must" in your specification.

Make Sure it's Realistic

1) For your project, you'll have to actually <u>make</u> the product according to the product specification — so all your requirements need to be things you're <u>capable</u> of producing.

2) Once you've got a product specification, you'll need to <u>compare</u> it to the design specification and confirm that each point is <u>satisfied</u>.

Some points will be <u>harder</u> to check than others. For example, if one of your design criteria is "must be very sweet", you'll have to actually make the product before you can check (by tasting) whether it's sweet enough. It's a good idea to take <u>photos</u> of any testing you do as evidence.

Billy realised that it was unrealistic to make sandwiches as big as him.

So many specifications, my head hurts, why why why...

If I told you that <u>product specifications</u> were going to get your pulse racing, I'd be lying. To be honest, they're a bit dull. But it's a vital step in <u>designing</u> and <u>manufacturing</u> a new product. So do it.

Planning Production

Plan How Long the Production Process Should Take

So you know just what you want to make — now you need to know how long it'll take.

You need to plan:
1) any <u>changes</u> needed to make it suitable for <u>mass-production</u>,
2) <u>how long</u> each stage will take,
3) what needs to be <u>prepared</u> before you can start each stage,
4) how you'll <u>ensure consistency</u> and <u>quality</u>.

Use Charts to Help You

You need to work out <u>what order</u> to do things in. It's important to work out <u>how long</u> each stage will take and how these times will fit into the <u>total time</u> you've allowed for production. You'll also have to take into account what <u>resources</u> you have, because doing tasks by hand usually takes longer.

① Work Order This can be produced as a <u>table</u> or <u>flow chart</u>. The purpose is to plan each task <u>in sequence</u>. You should include <u>quality control</u> checks. E.g. for making breaded chicken:

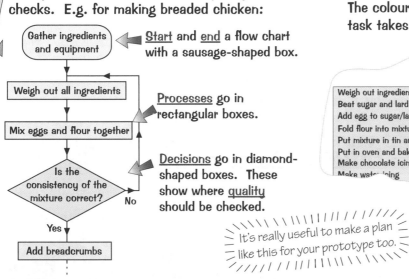

<u>Start</u> and <u>end</u> a flow chart with a sausage-shaped box.

<u>Processes</u> go in rectangular boxes.

<u>Decisions</u> go in diamond-shaped boxes. These show where <u>quality</u> should be checked.

It's really useful to make a plan like this for your prototype too.

② Gantt Chart This is a <u>time plan</u>. The tasks are listed <u>in order</u> down the <u>left-hand</u> side, and the <u>timing</u> plotted across the top. The coloured squares show <u>how long</u> each task takes. E.g. for making a cake:

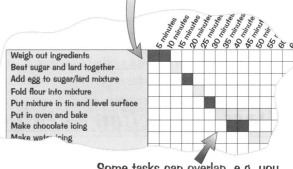

Some tasks can <u>overlap</u>, e.g. you can get on with making the icing while the cake is in the oven.

More <u>questionnaires</u> or <u>surveys</u> may help here. Ask people to give their opinions about the finished product — people in your target group if possible. <u>Record</u> your findings, e.g. using star profiles (see p47).

Test The Finished Product

When you think you've got the final product, it's vital to <u>photograph</u> and <u>test</u> it. You have to make sure it meets the original <u>design specification</u> (see p48) and your <u>product specification</u>.

Practice Questions

1) What is a <u>product specification</u>?
2) What do you need to <u>check</u> your product specification against?
3) How do each of these help your planning?   a) a <u>flow chart</u>
         b) a <u>Gantt Chart</u>
4) Make the following: a) a <u>flow chart</u> for <u>soft-boiling an egg</u>
         b) a <u>Gantt chart</u> for making <u>spaghetti bolognese</u>
5) What things should you <u>check</u> when you reckon you've got the <u>final product</u>?

Different Types of Production

Manufacturers use different methods of production depending on how many of a product they're making.

Job Production — Every Product's Unique

1) This is where you make a single product (it's also called 'craft production').
2) Every product's made differently to meet a specific request, e.g. a wedding cake.
3) Every product needs an individual recipe and an individual method.
4) Experienced workers with specialist skills are needed.
5) The products are high quality but they take a lot of time and cost a lot.

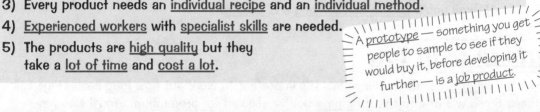

A prototype — something you get people to sample to see if they would buy it, before developing it further — is a job product.

Batch Production — Specified Quantities of a Product

1) This is where you make lots of your product in one go — each load you make is called a batch.
2) Every batch is made to meet specific requests from retailers, e.g. 100 chicken pies.
3) You can change batches to make another similar product, e.g. 500 steak pies.
4) But machines need to be cleaned between batches — this 'down time' is unproductive. Staff and machines need to be flexible so batches can be changed quickly, to avoid losing too much money.
5) Batch production is quicker than one-off production and it's a bit cheaper.
6) Workers can be less skilled but able to do lots of jobs well. Similar jobs (e.g. making a chicken or a steak pie) can be taken on, then modified for different types of pie.

Mass Production — Large Quantities of a Product

1) This is where you make large numbers of a product that sells well, e.g. a loaf of sliced bread.
2) The product's made using a production line — it passes through various stages of production. Products are made very quickly so they're cheap.
3) Machines are used at some of the stages so fewer workers are needed.
4) But to make a new product you need to change the production line — this can take a long time and this unproductive time costs money.
5) Workers are generally unskilled or low-skilled. They are trained to do one role and repeat it thousands of times, e.g. pouring filling into pastries.

Continuous Flow — Non-Stop Production 24hrs/day

1) This is where you make a product all the time, with no interruptions. It's basically non-stop mass production, with a production line using expensive, specialised equipment.
2) It's used for products that are sold regularly and in large numbers, e.g. baked beans.
3) It'd cost too much to keep turning equipment off and then re-starting it — so everything runs all the time. This keeps production costs really low.
4) But if anything goes wrong it takes time to get it going again, and unproductive time costs money.

A continuous flow of baked beans may produce side effects...

As usual, it's all about money. It's much cheaper for industries to produce something in huge numbers than one at a time — but it only works if the products are all the same and if they sell really well.

Different Types of Production

CAD Helps to Design Products...

1) This is where <u>computers</u> are used to help <u>design</u> a product.

2) You can use computer-aided design (<u>CAD</u>) to produce models of the <u>product</u> and its <u>packaging</u> in <u>2D</u> and <u>3D</u> — so you can view them from any angle.

3) Once the product's been drawn on screen, you can <u>easily recalculate values</u> and <u>change the design</u> until you're happy. CAD is <u>more accurate</u> and much <u>quicker</u> than drawing and re-drawing your designs on paper.

4) CAD is really useful to <u>calculate</u> things like your product's <u>nutritional value</u>, <u>portion size</u>, <u>shelf-life</u> and what it'll <u>cost</u> to make.

...and CAM Helps to Manufacture Them

<u>Computers</u> are used in the <u>manufacturing process</u> too — it's called computer-aided manufacture (<u>CAM</u>). Computers <u>control</u> some or all of the production stages, e.g. they're used to <u>weigh out</u> the <u>correct amount</u> of each ingredient, set the correct <u>oven temperature</u> and <u>cooking time</u>, etc. The whole production process is <u>overseen</u> by someone who keeps a close eye on everything.

Production <u>costs</u> are <u>lower</u> because <u>fewer staff</u> are needed.

CAM is <u>more accurate</u>, e.g. ingredients are weighed precisely — there's <u>less human error</u>.

Because machines are controlled by <u>computers</u>, staff don't need to go near <u>sharp blades</u>.

It can be <u>quicker</u> too — computers can make the production process <u>more efficient</u>.

Staff <u>don't</u> need to <u>handle</u> the food as much, making production <u>more hygienic</u>.

Products are <u>more consistent</u> — they're exactly the <u>same each time</u>.

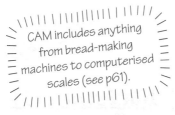

CAM includes anything from bread-making machines to computerised scales (see p61).

Practice Questions

1) Identify two <u>differences</u> between <u>job production</u> and <u>mass production</u>.

2) A cafe sells a range of sandwiches and usually sells about <u>1000 sandwiches per day</u>.
   a) Suggest what <u>method</u> of sandwich production would most suit the cafe and explain why.
   b) A customer wants to order a type of sandwich that isn't on the cafe's menu, so the owner agrees to make it for him. What is this method of production called?

3) A manufacturer decides to produce a breakfast cereal using <u>continuous flow</u>.
   a) What is continuous flow?
   b) Why might the manufacturer choose this method of production?
   c) Give one disadvantage of continuous flow.
   d) The cereal is produced using CAM. What does <u>CAM</u> stand for?
   e) Give two advantages for the manufacturer of using CAM.

4) Describe how using <u>CAD</u> helps a manufacturer to design their product.

Section Five — Production Processes

Shelf Life and Packaging

Shelf life is an important part of food safety — products that are past their shelf life might be dangerous.

The Shelf Life Tells You How Long Things Last

1) The shelf life of a product tells you how long you can keep it before it needs to be used. It's something you need to think about when you're designing a product.

2) Most commercial food products will have a shelf life, from fresh products like bread, to longer lasting ones like tinned tomatoes.

3) The shelf life is indicated by different dates (depending on the product):

Use by date

1) The use by date is shown on products with a short shelf life, e.g. high-risk foods (see below).

2) It's given as a safety warning. If you use the food after this date, it might not be safe — you run the risk of getting food poisoning as it's more likely to be contaminated by bacteria.

Best before date

1) The best before date is shown on products with a longer shelf life, e.g. tinned foods.

2) It's given as a warning about quality. If you eat the food after this date, it's probably safe but might not be as nice as you'd expect, e.g. biscuits could be soft.

Bacteria are the Main Cause of Food Poisoning

Products that are past their shelf life might be dangerous because of bacteria growing in them.

1) The symptoms of food poisoning include sickness, diarrhoea, stomach cramps and fever. In extreme cases, especially where people are old or vulnerable, it can lead to death.

2) The main cause of food poisoning is consuming food or drinks that are contaminated by bacteria — e.g. E. coli, salmonella and listeria. Bacteria are found everywhere — in air, water, people, animals, etc.

3) You can't see bacteria — they're so small you've got to use a microscope to spot them.

4) They often don't make the food look, taste or smell any different — so it's hard to know they're there.

5) Bacteria like conditions where they can multiply very quickly. These include:

• moisture   • warmth   • neutral pH

Food poisoning can also be caused by chemical or physical contamination — see p64.

Bacteria Grow Fastest in High-Risk Foods

High-risk foods are foods that bacteria grow quickly in, because they're moist and high in protein. High-risk foods include:

1) meat, fish and poultry
2) dairy products and eggs
3) gravies, stocks and sauces
4) shellfish and other seafood
5) cooked rice

EXAM TIP
You could get extra marks for naming high-risk foods and the types of bacteria that cause food poisoning.

High-risk foods often have a short shelf life — you can't keep them for long, or the bacteria can multiply to dangerous levels.

Baked bean curry — that's a high-risk food (to others)...

Knowing all this stuff will help you through your GCSE and it'll save your stomach loads of grief — so it must be worth it. Learn the examples of high-risk foods and the bacteria that can make you ill.

Shelf Life and Packaging

Packaging _can_ Extend Shelf Life

❶ MODIFIED ATMOSPHERE PACKAGING (MAP)

MAP extends the shelf life of <u>fresh foods</u>, e.g. fresh and cooked meats, fresh pasta, cheese and sandwiches.

1) The food is put into <u>plastic</u> packaging with a mixture of <u>oxygen</u>, <u>nitrogen</u> and <u>carbon dioxide</u> in particular proportions. It's then <u>sealed</u> and <u>chilled</u>.

2) But once the packet's been <u>opened</u>, the food has a <u>normal shelf life</u>.

❷ VACUUM PACKAGING

Vacuum packaging is often used for dry foods, e.g. <u>coffee</u>, and for <u>meat</u> and <u>fish</u>.

1) Food is put into plastic packaging, then the air is <u>sucked away</u> from around the food. It's then <u>sealed</u> to keep the food in <u>oxygen-free</u> conditions.

2) Once the packet is <u>open</u> you have to follow the storage instructions.

❸ CANNING

Canning is used for <u>processed foods</u>, e.g. baked beans, cooked meat, soup, etc.

1) <u>Heat</u> is used to kill any <u>bacteria</u> (see next page).

2) The can is <u>sealed</u>, and whatever's inside lasts for <u>ages</u> (as nothing can <u>get in</u> to spoil it).

Nanotechnology _can_ Improve Packaging Properties

Nanotechnology is a <u>new technology</u> that involves using <u>very, very small particles</u> (<u>nanoparticles</u>).

1) Some nanoparticles can make packaging <u>stronger</u>, <u>lighter</u> or more <u>heat-resistant</u>.

2) Food can be made to <u>last longer</u>, e.g. adding <u>clay nanoparticles</u> to plastic makes the packaging better at keeping out oxygen and moisture. Some nanoparticles can <u>kill</u> harmful bacteria.

3) '<u>Smart materials</u>' change depending on the <u>conditions</u>, like pressure, light, temperature, etc.

4) <u>Smart packaging</u> can use <u>nanoparticles</u> to <u>change</u> the packaging's <u>properties</u>, e.g. meat packaging that <u>changes colour</u> when the <u>temperature</u> gets too <u>high</u> (like if it's been out the fridge for too long).

Practice Questions

1) How is a <u>use by date</u> different from a <u>best before date</u>?

2) Give three symptoms of <u>food poisoning</u>.

3) Name three types of <u>bacteria</u> that can cause food poisoning.

4) Describe the <u>three conditions</u> that allow bacteria to multiply very quickly.

5) Name two conditions that make <u>high-risk foods</u> ideal for bacteria.

6) Name <u>four</u> high-risk foods.

7) Emma wants to set up a business making and selling <u>sandwiches</u>. She is considering what type of packaging to use.
   a) Suggest a packaging technique she could use to keep the sandwiches fresh.
   b) Outline the process used to package food this way.

8) Name two products than could be <u>packaged</u> in:
   a) Modified Atmosphere Packaging
   b) vacuum packaging
   c) cans

9) Give two ways in which <u>nanotechnology</u> can be used in packaging to make food last longer.

Preservation and Additives

Cooking and storing foods at the correct <u>temperatures</u> can extend their <u>shelf life</u> and make them <u>safe</u> to eat. <u>Additives</u> also help preserve food, as well as <u>enhancing colour</u> and <u>flavour</u>.

You can Change the Temperature to Preserve Food

Cook food ABOVE 72 °C to KILL bacteria

1) <u>Canning</u> — food is put into a sealed can and <u>heated</u> to <u>115 °C</u>, killing any bacteria. Because the can is <u>sealed</u>, no more bacteria can get in.

2) <u>UHT</u> (Ultra Heat Treatment) — <u>milk</u> is <u>heated</u> to really high temperatures (between <u>132 °C</u> and <u>140 °C</u>) for 1-2 seconds. It's then <u>cooled rapidly</u> and <u>packaged</u>. Unopened UHT milk can be kept for <u>months</u>.

DEHYDRATING food stops bacteria from growing

<u>Dehydration</u> means <u>drying</u> something to <u>remove</u> all the <u>moisture</u> so bacteria can't grow. There are different <u>methods</u>, like <u>sun drying</u>, <u>air drying</u> and <u>kiln drying</u>, which work at <u>different temperatures</u>.

Chill at 0 °C to 5 °C to SLOW the growth of bacteria

1) Keeping food in the <u>fridge</u>, between <u>0 °C and 5 °C</u>, <u>slows</u> down the growth of bacteria.

2) This <u>extends</u> the <u>shelf life</u> of the food — although it won't last as long as canned or bottled foods do.

3) <u>High-risk</u> foods <u>MUST</u> be kept chilled to prevent the risk of <u>food poisoning</u>.

4) Chilling food doesn't change its properties much — chilled food <u>looks</u> and <u>tastes</u> the <u>same</u> — but it may have a <u>harder texture</u>.

°C

— 80
— 70
— 60
— 50
— 40
— 30
— 20
— 10
— 0
— –10
— –20

COOK CHILL products last for up to 5 days

1) Products are <u>cooked</u> then <u>chilled</u> (to between <u>0 °C and 3 °C</u>) within <u>90 minutes</u>.

2) They're stored in a fridge (between <u>0 °C and 5 °C</u>) for up to 5 days.

3) They should be <u>reheated</u> (to above <u>72 °C</u>) before being eaten. They <u>can't</u> then be reheated again.

Bacteria grow and multiply quickly in the DANGER ZONE — 5 °C to 63 °C

Freeze food at –18 °C to STOP THE GROWTH of bacteria

1) Freezing food at <u>–18 °C</u> or lower <u>stops bacteria growing</u> — they become <u>dormant</u>.

2) Freezing <u>greatly extends</u> the <u>shelf life</u> of the food and the <u>nutrients aren't lost</u>.

3) It <u>doesn't kill</u> the bacteria though. They become <u>active</u> again when the food defrosts.

Danger Zones — exam halls...

What a shame you can't preserve your revision. You could learn a page, pop the know-it-all section of your brain into the freezer and then get it out again for your exam. Oh, but better defrost it fully first...

Preservation and Additives

Additives are Really Useful Substances Added to Food

1) An additive is something that's added to a food product to improve its properties.

2) Some additives occur naturally and some are made artificially. Customers tend to prefer the idea of natural additives, so manufacturers try to use these where possible.

3) All additives must pass a safety test before they can be used in food. When an additive passes it gets an E number, meaning it can be used throughout the European Union, e.g. caramel colouring is E150a.

Additives have lots of Uses...

1) Preservatives are additives that prevent bacteria from growing — so the food has a longer shelf life.

- Salt — salt absorbs water from bacteria, making them shrivel up and die. Salt is used to preserve meats like ham — but it makes food taste salty.
- Sugar — using high amounts of sugar (e.g. in jam) kills bacteria in much the same way. But then of course the food tastes very sweet.

- Vinegar — vinegar is too acidic for bacteria to grow (they need a neutral pH — 6.5 to 7.5). This gives food an acidic, tangy taste and can make it look brown. It's used in chutneys and pickles.
- Concentrated lemon juice — lemon juice is also acidic. It's used to preserve fruit salads.

2) Colourings make food look more attractive and appealing to eat, e.g. tartrazine (a yellow colour). They can also be used to return food to its natural colour if the colour's lost during processing.

3) Flavourings improve the taste or the aroma (smell) of a product, e.g. vanilla, herbs and spices.

4) Flavour and colour enhancers in nanoparticles (see p57) can improve the taste and look of some foods. Nanoparticles can also be used as emulsifiers or setting agents to improve the texture of food.

...but they have Disadvantages Too

1) Some people are allergic to certain additives and can react badly to them — kids tend to react more than adults.

2) Some additives can be bad for our health if used in large amounts, e.g. sugar and salt.

3) They can disguise poor quality ingredients, e.g. processed meat products may not contain much meat but they can be made to taste good by using additives.

4) Some people think eating additives could be linked to behavioural problems, e.g. studies are looking at whether a colouring additive called sunset yellow is linked to hyperactive behaviour in children.

Practice Questions

1) Describe the cook chill process.

2) What is the danger zone?

3) What temperature should you freeze food at?

4) Describe how these additives preserve food:
   a) salt
   b) vinegar

5) Give three disadvantages of using additives.

Tools and Equipment

A bad workman always blames his tools. Or is it a bad chef who always blames his whisk?
Anyway, you've got loads of top tools to make use of in Food Technology...

Different Tasks Need Different Tools

To make a good product, you need to be able to select the right equipment and be able to use it safely.

WEIGHING AND MEASURING

1) You need to be able to weigh and measure ingredients accurately.

2) Weighing scales (electronic and balance scales) are used to weigh dry ingredients (e.g. flour) and solid ingredients like butter.

3) Liquids are measured in measuring jugs or cups (some dry ingredients are measured in cups too).

4) You can use measuring spoons for small amounts of ingredients.

CUTTING

1) You use different knives depending on what you're cutting, e.g. bread or cheese knives.

2) A mandolin can be used to slice and cut foods evenly.

3) You can use pastry cutters to cut out the same size and shape every time.

MIXING

1) The tools you use for mixing depend on what you're mixing and the quantities you're using.

2) There are different ways of mixing ingredients — e.g. blending, folding, whisking, etc. (see p19).

3) For mixing fairly small amounts of ingredients, you can mix by hand using a spoon or a whisk. But mixing by hand can be hard work and take ages, and won't always give a smooth, consistent mixture.

4) Hand-held mixers and blenders save time and effort, and produce more consistent results.

5) Food processors can be used for mixing, slicing, chopping or dicing food. Using the same settings will give you the same results each time.

6) In industrial food production, floor-standing mixers are used — they're large food processors that can mix huge quantities of ingredients.

SHAPING

1) You often need to be able to shape your ingredients.

2) You can do this by hand, e.g. shaping dough into biscuits. Your results won't be very consistent — there'll be lots of different shapes and sizes.

3) Cutters can help you make more consistent shapes.

4) You can use moulds to set liquids into different shapes (e.g. jelly).

HEATING AND COOLING

1) There are lots of different ways you can heat things up. You can use ovens, hobs, microwaves and steamers — it all depends on what you want to cook.

2) You can check that things have been heated to the right temperature by using a thermometer or temperature probe, which measures the temperature inside the food. You should use a probe with high-risk foods (like meats — see p56) to check they're properly cooked.

3) Industrial ovens are usually computer-controlled and bigger than the ones you'd use at home or at school. Examples include tunnel ovens, deck ovens and travel ovens.

4) You use refrigerators to cool things down and freezers to freeze things (fairly obvious really).

Cooking by radiator takes an awfully long time...

Make sure you know which tools you can use for each task — and the best ones to use when you're making your product. A lot of it's quite straightforward — I'm sure you know that knives chop things.

Tools and Equipment

Using Electrical Equipment can Improve Your Product

1) Electrical equipment is any piece of <u>equipment</u> that works using <u>electricity</u> (from the mains or batteries).
2) It's much <u>quicker</u> and <u>easier</u> to use electrical equipment (e.g. for whisking) than doing things by hand.
3) It should work the <u>same way every time</u> — so you get <u>consistent results</u>.
4) You get a <u>quality product</u> because of more <u>accurate</u> and <u>precise</u> measurements and timings.

Example: Weighing Scales

1) <u>Computerised scales</u> are more <u>accurate</u> than <u>balance scales</u>.
2) They'll <u>weigh ingredients precisely</u> to within <u>0.05 g</u>.
3) There's <u>less</u> room for <u>human error</u> in reading a digital display than with judging when balance pans are level (or when a needle is pointing to the right number).
4) You can <u>preset</u> the scales to weigh different ingredients, so they're more accurate. This <u>saves time</u> — products which are <u>underweight or overweight</u> can then be <u>rejected</u>.
5) They can be <u>linked</u> to a <u>computer</u> so that <u>feedback</u> is <u>immediate</u> (e.g. no more ingredients are added when a certain weight is reached) — they're often used in CAM (see p55).

Practice Questions

1) What equipment would you use to <u>measure</u>:
   a) flour?
   b) milk?
2) What is a <u>mandolin</u> used for?
3) Name three different pieces of equipment you might use for <u>mixing</u>.
4) What is a <u>disadvantage</u> of shaping ingredients by <u>hand</u>?

5) Look at this lovely <u>jelly</u>. What piece of <u>equipment</u> has been used to get the jelly to be this fetching shape?
6) Name four different pieces of equipment used to <u>heat</u> things.
7) What is a <u>temperature probe</u> used for?
8) Describe how <u>industrial ovens</u> are different from ones you'd use at home or at school.
9) Describe what you'd use the following bits of equipment for:
   a) a knife
   b) a food processor
   c) a cutter
   d) a steamer
10) Why is using <u>electrical equipment</u> generally better for <u>mixing</u> than doing it by hand?
11) Give three advantages of using <u>computerised scales</u>.
12) Why should you not stick your hand in a <u>blender</u> while it's switched on?

Safety and Quality Checking

It's dead important that you use equipment <u>safely</u> — you don't want to lose any fingers.

Use Equipment Safely and Hygienically

1) Always <u>read the instructions</u> carefully before using equipment and use equipment <u>efficiently</u>.

2) Everyone should <u>wash their hands</u> both <u>before</u> and <u>after</u> using equipment. All <u>equipment</u> needs to be <u>thoroughly cleaned</u> too — this prevents <u>cross-contamination</u> (when <u>bacteria</u> are passed from one thing to another, e.g. bacteria from <u>raw</u> meat or off people's <u>hands</u>).

3) Workers should be given appropriate <u>health and safety training</u> — e.g. being told how to use <u>safety guards</u> and <u>emergency stop buttons</u>. Equipment should be <u>regularly serviced</u>. Workers should also have <u>appropriate health and safety qualifications</u> — e.g. <u>food hygiene certificates</u>.

Follow Safety and Hygiene Procedures at Every Step

PREPARING FOOD
- Follow <u>personal hygiene procedures</u> — <u>wash your hands</u>, wear a clean <u>apron</u>, wear a <u>hat</u> or <u>hair net</u>, remove all <u>jewellery</u>, cover all <u>cuts</u>, report to the person in charge if you're <u>ill</u> and don't taste food with your <u>fingers</u>.
- Always use <u>clean equipment</u> to <u>avoid cross-contamination</u>.
- If you're <u>defrosting</u> frozen food before cooking it, make sure it's defrosted <u>fully</u>.

COOKING FOOD
- <u>Cook</u> food <u>thoroughly</u> to <u>kill bacteria</u> — the temperature of the food should be <u>72 °C</u> or more in the middle. (It should be <u>reheated</u> to the same temperature for at least <u>three minutes</u>.)
- Make sure food is <u>cooked all the way through</u>, e.g. cook <u>thicker</u> pieces of meat for <u>longer</u> than thin ones — <u>test the middle</u> to make sure they're cooked properly.
- If you're keeping food <u>warm</u>, keep it at about <u>70 °C</u>, and don't keep things warm for <u>more than an hour</u> before eating.

TRANSPORTING FOOD
- Food should be transported <u>quickly</u> and <u>securely</u> — so that products stay <u>fresh</u> and aren't <u>damaged</u> by bumps.
- Make sure food is transported at the <u>right temperature</u>, e.g. in <u>refrigerated trucks</u>.
- Avoid <u>cross-contamination</u> — transport raw and cooked products <u>separately</u>.
- Make sure all transportation equipment is <u>clean</u>.

STORING FOOD
- Always <u>follow the storage instructions</u> — especially <u>temperature</u> instructions.
- Use older purchases <u>before</u> they go <u>out of date</u>.
- Keep food <u>sealed</u> or <u>covered up</u> once it's opened.

An EHO Checks Things are Safe and Hygienic

1) <u>Environmental Health Officers</u> (EHOs) <u>maintain</u> and <u>improve</u> public <u>health standards</u> — things like checking <u>food hygiene</u> and making sure <u>health and safety regulations</u> are being followed.

2) In the <u>food industry</u>, this means checking that food <u>storage</u>, <u>preparation</u> and <u>sale</u> areas are <u>clean</u> and <u>safe</u> to work in, and that the food produced is <u>safe to eat</u>.

This page is contaminated...

Make sure you know how to use equipment <u>safely</u> — a lot of it's just common sense, like don't put your hand in a blender. Remember how to keep things <u>hygienic</u> and avoid <u>cross-contamination</u>.

Safety and Quality Checking

Mass-Produced Products need to be Consistent

Manufacturers who make products on a large scale aim to produce consistent products —
products that are the same every time, e.g. they have the same taste, colour, portion size, etc.
Customers can rely on the product being just like the one they liked before.

> QUALITY ASSURANCE (QA) is all about standards — setting standards and meeting them.
> QUALITY CONTROL (QC) is how you check whether you're meeting those standards (see below).

Products are Checked by Using Quality Control

Manufacturers set standards that their products must meet (quality assurance) and they check to make sure
these standards are being met — this is quality control. Checks are made at every stage of production and
the final product is checked too. A series of quality controls make up a quality assurance process.

1) Visual checks
   - The colour of the product is checked against a standard colour.
   - The packaging is checked to make sure it's not damaged and all the labels are clearly printed.
2) Testing
   - Samples are tasted at the end, to make sure the taste is exactly what the manufacturer wants.
   - The size, thickness and pH of the product may also be tested.

Any Problems are Fed Back Straight Away

There's no point in a manufacturer doing all this checking unless any problems are then corrected.
1) If a product's not right, the problem is relayed back to the factory floor — this is called feedback.
2) Feedback happens straight away so the problem can be fixed quickly.
3) This means ingredients aren't wasted — so the manufacturer saves time and money.

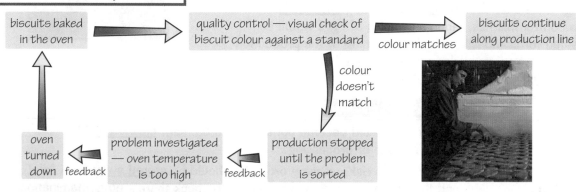

EXAMPLE — biscuit production

biscuits baked in the oven → quality control — visual check of biscuit colour against a standard → colour matches → biscuits continue along production line

colour doesn't match

oven turned down ← *feedback* ← problem investigated — oven temperature is too high ← *feedback* ← production stopped until the problem is sorted

Practice Questions

1) What is cross-contamination?

2) Describe how to keep things safe and hygienic when:
   a) preparing food
   b) transporting food

3) What does an Environmental Health Officer do?

4) Describe Quality Assurance and Quality Control.

HACCP

Risk assessment and HACCP are important in food production — and they might just come up in your exam.

Risk Assessment is all about Hazards and Risks

HAZARD
Anything that could cause harm or problems during the making, packaging, storing or transport of a product is a hazard.

RISK The risk is the likelihood of that hazard actually causing a problem.

3 Tons

RISK ASSESSMENT
Risk assessment means thinking about: what could happen, when it could happen, and what steps are needed to reduce the risk. It applies to both food hygiene and the safety of workers.

HACCP Helps Avoid Food Contamination

It's important that products won't harm the consumer. HACCP helps identify potential problems and put controls in place to prevent food being contaminated before it reaches the consumer.

Hazard Analysis Critical Control Points (HACCP)

A **HAZARD** is anything that's likely to cause harm.

ANALYSIS is when you look in detail at something.

CRITICAL means it's very serious.

A **CONTROL POINT** is a step in the process where you put in a control to prevent a problem from occurring.

There are three types of contamination that HACCP tries to stop:

BIOLOGICAL contamination

The product could become contaminated by bacteria, especially if it contains high-risk foods (see p56). E.g. there's a risk that eggs could carry salmonella. To control this risk, random samples of eggs would be tested for salmonella near the beginning of the production process. You could also take samples of the end product, e.g. quiche, to be extra cautious.

I couldn't find a photo of salmonella bacteria, so here's a good-looking young chap on a bike instead. Much nicer anyway.

CHEMICAL contamination

1) The product could become contaminated by, say, cleaning fluids during storage or processing.

2) To control this risk, cleaning products should be stored away from food and the final product should be tested to check there's no contamination.

PHYSICAL contamination

1) The product could become contaminated by physical objects, e.g. bits of jewellery, chipped nail varnish, hair, insects, etc.

2) To control these risks, workers wear overalls and hairnets, with no jewellery or nail varnish allowed, and food is kept covered as much as possible. Finished products are also checked.

I know I am, I'm sure I am — I'm HACCP...

There's a whole pile of words and initials to remember here, but the principle is pretty simple. Identify hazards, work out the risk of these hazards happening, then try to reduce these risks.

HACCP

Set up HACCP Step by Step

1) In rough, write down how you're going to make your product in a series of steps.

2) Think about your product from 'field to table', i.e. consider the stages your ingredients will go through, from the beginning (before they're harvested) to the end (when the product's bought by the consumer).

3) Use a simple flow chart to set out the steps that you've identified.

4) Then consider any potential hazards associated with each step. For example:

   a) The production or purchase of the ingredients — you need to make sure you get high quality ingredients from a reliable source.

   b) Storage of ingredients — e.g. make sure dry ingredients aren't kept in damp conditions.

   c) The actual making process (this is the most important area for HACCP).

   d) Packaging — e.g. make sure the packaging doesn't damage the product.

   e) Transport from factory to shop — check it's being transported at the right temperature and won't get damaged.

5) Finally, you have to think about how you can control and prevent problems from taking place.

Example: HACCP for a Decorated Cake

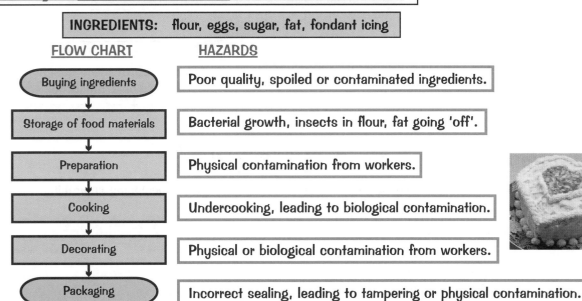

INGREDIENTS: flour, eggs, sugar, fat, fondant icing

FLOW CHART   **HAZARDS**

FLOW CHART	HAZARDS
Buying ingredients	Poor quality, spoiled or contaminated ingredients.
Storage of food materials	Bacterial growth, insects in flour, fat going 'off'.
Preparation	Physical contamination from workers.
Cooking	Undercooking, leading to biological contamination.
Decorating	Physical or biological contamination from workers.
Packaging	Incorrect sealing, leading to tampering or physical contamination.

Once you've identified the hazards and risks, you can work out what to do — how to stop them or control them. These would be your control points. (See, it's easy when you know how.)

Practice Questions

1) Describe:
   a) a hazard
   b) a risk
   c) a risk assessment

2) What does HACCP stand for? Why do manufacturers use HACCP?

3) Name the three different types of contamination.

4) Describe how you can avoid each of the three types of contamination that HACCP tries to prevent.

5) Describe how you'd set up a HACCP.

Exam Technique

1) The exam is made up of <u>2 papers</u>. The first is on '<u>Sustainable Design</u>' — it's one hour long.

2) This paper is about all the things you have to consider when designing a product — including all the stages of the <u>design process</u> and the <u>environmental</u> and <u>social</u> considerations.

The Sustainable Design Paper Has Two Parts...

...Section A has 15 Short Answer Questions...

This'll contain <u>multiple choice</u> questions, <u>true and false</u> questions and some questions where you have to <u>write</u> a few words.

> Section A is worth <u>15</u> out of the 60 marks on the paper.

---

1   A fair trade product is one that:

  (a) can be recycled

  (b) is made in a less economically developed country

  (c) is made using sustainable resources

  (d) is made by people who are paid fairly   **[1]**

Decide whether this statement is *true* or *false*.

                                    True   False

2   Mass production requires a large number of skilled workers. ☐ ☐ **[1]**

3   What is the name given to a material that rots naturally in the environment?

    ....**[1]**

> Read <u>all</u> the answers — don't just go for the first one that sounds possible.

> If you <u>don't know</u> the answer to a multiple choice, you might as well <u>guess</u>. You won't lose a mark and you might get lucky.

> Don't spend more than <u>a minute</u> on each of these questions — there's only <u>1 mark</u> for each.

...Section B Contains The Design Questions

You'll have to write <u>longer answers</u> in this section. It'll also involve you <u>designing something</u>...

---

4 (a) Design a new high-energy snack that meets the following specification:

  • contains a lot of carbohydrates and sugar,

  • uses ethically produced ingredients,

  • can be eaten 'on the go'.

Use sketches and notes to show your initial ideas for your chosen product. Do not draw the packaging. **[6]**

Design 1
Oat bar with chocolate topping

use fair trade chocolate

oats are a good source of carbohydrates

Design 2 Cookie with dried fruit and nut pieces

small enough to fit in a pocket

Design 3 Summer fruit muffin

use locally-grown fruit

cake is a good source of carbohydrates and sugar

use fair trade dried fruit

> You need to produce a <u>range</u> of ideas — but you don't have time to go overboard. <u>Three</u> is a good number.

> To get the full 6 marks you need to <u>colour</u> your sketches in and <u>annotate</u> them to explain your ideas. Be as <u>creative</u> as you can.

> Also make sure each design idea is <u>different</u> from the others — you won't get marks if they're too similar.

Exam Technique

(b) Use notes and sketches to develop one of your initial ideas.
[5]

Design 1

Fruits from local farms, which reduce food miles and support local producers.

Chocolate topping made using fair trade chocolate, which is ethical because it gives workers in LEDCs a fair price and good working conditions.

The oats, the chocolate and the syrup will make it high in carbohydrates and sugar.

The oats will be held together using golden syrup and margarine, so it won't crumble or fall apart — this will make it easier to eat 'on the go'.

The bar will be made from oats with some dried fruits added. The fruits will provide fibre, carbohydrates and vitamins B and C.

> Make it really, really clear how your design <u>matches</u> each point in the <u>specification</u>. That's what the examiners will be looking for.

> Check you've covered <u>all</u> the points in the design specification. It helps if you <u>tick off</u> each one as you go.

> You need to <u>develop</u> your initial idea. Add some <u>extra features</u> to make it match the specification more closely. If you have time, <u>colour</u> it in.

(c) Explain two ways you could lessen the environmental impact of how your product is made.

1. The ingredients could be bought from local sources, to reduce the pollution caused by transporting them.

2. The bar could be baked using the most efficient cooking method, e.g. bake as many bars as possible in a fan-assisted oven or convection microwave. These cook things quicker and reduce the energy needed. **[4]**

> This question's worth <u>4 marks</u> — you'll get <u>1 mark</u> for each <u>idea</u>, and <u>1 mark</u> for <u>explaining</u> each one.

> You might not be asked to actually <u>design</u> the <u>packaging</u>, but you will have to think about it — like what <u>materials</u> to use.

(d) (i) The packaging for this product has to be recyclable. Suggest one suitable material for your product.

Recyclable plastic. **[1]**

> This whole paper is called '<u>Sustainable Design</u>' — so you can bet your last pair of clean undies that they'll ask you about the sustainability of <u>your</u> design.
>
> Bear your product's <u>eco footprint</u> in mind right from the start.

(ii) Recycling is one way to make packaging more sustainable. With reference to the 6Rs, give two other ways in which you could make the packaging for your product more sustainable.

1. <u>Reduce</u> the amount of packaging used and make sure you don't have excess packaging.

2. <u>Refuse</u> to use materials that come from an unsustainable source, e.g. paper made from wood that comes from an unsustainable plantation. **[4]**

> It's likely that part of a question will be on the <u>6Rs</u> (see p32-33) — make sure you know what they are and how they relate to <u>packaging</u>, <u>diet</u> and <u>nutrition</u>.

Exam Technique

And Now for the 'Technical Aspects' Paper

1) The second paper is on 'Technical Aspects of Designing and Making' — it's 1 hour 15 minutes long.

2) It's also made up of two sections...

...Section A is Just Technical Stuff...

It'll ask you about ingredients and equipment.

> Section A is made up of three questions.

1 Cakes are often made by combining flour, eggs, butter and sugar.

> You'll need to know a bit about health and safety issues for this paper — things like spotting and preventing hazards.

(a) Flour and sugar are both good sources of carbohydrate. Give **one** function of carbohydrate in the diet.

Carbohydrates provide us with energy. ....[1]

> This one's only worth one mark, so you don't have to write very much.

(b) One part of the cake making process is to cream together the two ingredients. Describe the creaming method, naming the ingredients and any equipment involved.

Creaming is mixing together butter and sugar into

a creamy mixture. It traps air bubbles to make the

cake rise. You can do it by hand, e.g. using a wooden

spoon or by using a mixer or food processor. **[3]**

> Underline the key words in the question to help you focus. Here you need to write about the creaming method.

> Look to see how many lines there are — this is a good guide for how long your answer should be.

(c) The cake mixture is then baked in an oven.

(i) What method of heat transfer takes place when baking?

Convection ....[1]

> Some questions only need a one-word answer.

(ii) Briefly describe how fan-assisted ovens work, and give **one** advantage of using a fan-assisted oven.

In a fan-assisted oven, the hot air is circulated

by a fan. This is good because it means food

cooks more evenly as all parts of the oven are

the same temperature. ....[2]

> 'Briefly describe' means you don't need to go into too much detail. There are two marks, one for the description and one for the advantage, so neither have to be very detailed.

Exam Technique

...Section B is About Design, Sustainability and Human Use

Pretty much <u>anything</u> can come up in this section, but one of the questions is likely to ask you to <u>modify</u> a food product in some way.

Section B is made up of <u>two questions</u>.

4   A test kitchen has carried out sensory testing on two pies. Both pies had exactly the same fillings but their pastry was different.
The star profiles below show the results.

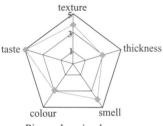

Pie made using home-made pastry.

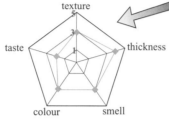

Pie made using a standard component pastry.

Look <u>carefully</u> at the star profiles and make sure you <u>understand</u> what they show — don't rush straight into answering the question.

(a) Analyse the results and suggest how they might be used by the manufacturers.

The sensory tests show that people preferred the
taste, texture and smell of the home-made pastry
but they preferred the thickness of the standard
component pastry. Overall, the home-made pie
scored higher marks, especially for the taste, so it's
more likely to be popular with consumers.
Manufacturers could use these results to develop
a new pastry which has the best qualities of
both.   [4]

<u>Analyse</u> means you need to <u>describe</u> what the data shows and <u>draw some conclusions</u>.

The <u>number of lines</u> you're given for your answer is a big clue to <u>how much</u> you should write (as well as the number of <u>marks</u>).

Do <u>everything</u> that the question asks — don't forget to say how the sensory tests may be used by <u>manufacturers</u> too.

(b) Give a reason why standard components are used in food production.

They save the manufacturer time.   [1]

The question is only worth <u>one mark</u> so you only need to put <u>one reason</u>.

(c)* People with coeliac disease can't eat gluten. Explain how you would modify a pie to be suitable for people with coeliac disease.

I would experiment with gluten-free flour and
adjusting the cooking times, to make pastry...

The asterix (*) means you can get marks for <u>good written communication</u> in this question. So make sure you check your <u>spelling</u>, <u>grammar</u> and <u>punctuation</u>.

When you think you've <u>finished</u> the exam, go back and <u>read over</u> your answers to check for <u>mistakes</u>. You might even think of something else you could <u>add</u> and pick up some <u>extra marks</u>.

Mud Pie

If you're ever stuck for dessert ideas, try a mud pie. It's cheap, it's easy to make and it's low in fat.

First, You Have to Source Your Ingredients

The two basic ingredients of any mud pie are soil and water. But there are lots of different places you can get your ingredients from — and they'll all have a slightly different flavour. As with all products, it's important to consider the environmental impact of your pie as well.

Soil from your own garden (well, probably your parents' garden) — this has the advantage of being a local product, so its food miles will be pretty low. However, if your garden isn't in a very good state, the soil might not be very tasty, and could be contaminated with things like slugs.

Soil from your neighbour's garden — of course, if your garden isn't very nice, you can always try soil from your neighbour's garden. This has similar advantages to using soil from your own garden — but your neighbours might not be too happy with you digging up their flower beds.

Organic soil (see p38 for more on organic food) — organic soil won't have been treated with any nasty chemicals, so it's better for the environment. However, it's quite expensive, so check and see if the soil in your garden can be classed as organic.

Manure — err, on second thoughts, maybe not.

There are lots of different types of water to choose from, e.g. tap water, mineral water, rain water, stream water and sea water. Try them all, and see which type you prefer. Remember, if you use sea water, your pie have a higher salt content.

Mud Pies are Dead Easy to Make

There's lots of trial and error involved in pie-making, and a lot of it's down to personal preference. Here are the basic steps:

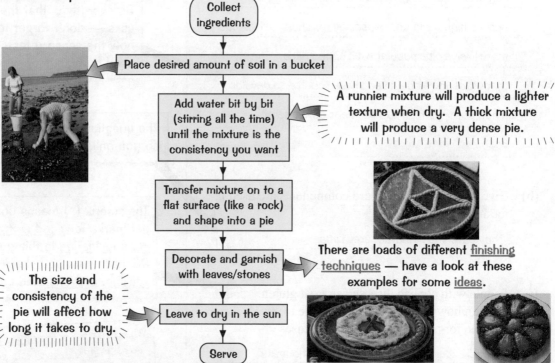

Collect ingredients

Place desired amount of soil in a bucket

Add water bit by bit (stirring all the time) until the mixture is the consistency you want

A runnier mixture will produce a lighter texture when dry. A thick mixture will produce a very dense pie.

Transfer mixture on to a flat surface (like a rock) and shape into a pie

Decorate and garnish with leaves/stones

There are loads of different finishing techniques — have a look at these examples for some ideas.

The size and consistency of the pie will affect how long it takes to dry.

Leave to dry in the sun

Serve

I'm sure you'll muddle through...

It's best to make your pie on a sunny day — otherwise it'll take ages to dry and you could be waiting for days. And if you do it on a rainy day, there's a risk your pie will be washed away.

Glossary

5 a day	The Government recommends that everyone should eat at least five portions of different <u>fruits or vegetables</u> every day in order to be healthy.
6Rs	<u>Recycle</u>, <u>Reuse</u>, <u>Reduce</u>, <u>Refuse</u>, <u>Rethink</u>, <u>Repair</u>.
additive	Something that's added to a food product to improve its properties.
aerate	To <u>add air</u> to a mixture to help make it lighter, e.g. when making cakes.
aesthetics	How a product <u>looks</u>, <u>tastes</u>, <u>smells</u>, etc.
alternative protein	A form of protein other than protein from meat (e.g. tofu, TVP), which is suitable for vegetarians.
amino acids	<u>Proteins</u> are made of amino acids.
balanced diet	A <u>healthy diet</u> that contains a bit of everything your body needs.
batch production	Making a certain number of a product in one go.
binding	<u>Holding ingredients together</u> so the product doesn't fall apart. For example, eggs are used to bind ingredients in burgers.
biodegradable	A biodegradable material is something that <u>rots down</u> naturally.
CAD	Computer-aided design.
CAM	Computer-aided manufacture.
carbon footprint	A measure of the impact something has on the environment, based on the harmful <u>greenhouse gases</u> produced.
closed question	A question with a limited number of possible answers, e.g. do you like spicy food?
coagulate	To change into a <u>more solid</u> state. For example, if you fry an egg it coagulates.
conduction	The transfer of energy through <u>solids</u>.
consistent	The <u>same</u> every time.
contaminate	To make something dirty or unhygienic, e.g. a fly could contaminate your soup.
continuous flow	Continuous flow production means making large numbers of a product <u>non-stop</u>.
control point	A stage in a process where you put in a control to stop a problem occurring.
convection	The transfer of energy through <u>gases</u> (e.g. air) or <u>liquids</u>.
cross-contamination	Transferring potentially harmful bacteria from one thing to another, e.g. via work surfaces, equipment or your hands.

Glossary

danger zone	The range of temperatures (5 °C to 63 °C) in which bacteria multiply very quickly.
deficiency	Not getting enough of something, e.g. calcium deficiency.
design brief	A short statement explaining why there's a need for a new product.
design specification	The general characteristics a product should have, e.g. appealing to children. The design specification is usually made up of a list of design criteria.
deteriorate	When the quality of food decreases or it 'goes off'.
disassembly	Taking a product apart and examining the bits.
E number	A number (e.g. E150a) given to an additive when it passes EU safety tests. The additive can then be used in food throughout the European Union.
eco footprint	A measure of the human demands on environmental resources.
emulsifier	Something that keeps an oily and watery mixture stable (stops it separating).
emulsion	A mixture of oily and watery liquids, e.g. salad dressing.
enriching	Adding something like butter or cream to a product to make it thicker and tastier.
Environmental Health Officer (EHO)	A person who monitors public and environmental health standards, e.g. by doing routine hygiene inspections.
essential amino acids	Amino acids that the body can't make itself so you need to get them from your diet.
ethical issue	A moral issue — when many people have views about whether something's morally right or wrong, e.g. battery farming.
Ethical Trading Initiative (ETI)	The ETI helps workers in developing countries get fair wages and good working conditions.
fair trade	When workers in developing countries get a fair price for their food and have good working conditions.
feedback	Sending back information during production, often so that a person or a computer can monitor whether a process is working as it should.
fermentation	When yeast breaks down sugars to release carbon dioxide and alcohol.
finishing techniques	Techniques that are used to make the finished product look as good as possible, e.g. glazing, icing, garnishing.
food miles	The distance a product travels from where it's produced or grown to where it's sold.
food scares	When a particular food is linked to a health problem — often people stop buying it.

Glossary

fortification	When <u>extra nutrients</u> are added to a food or drink.
fossil fuels	<u>Coal</u>, <u>oil</u> and <u>natural gas</u>, or fuels made from them, e.g. petrol.
free-range	Free-range animals have <u>more space</u> to live — they're <u>free to roam</u>.
Gantt chart	A time plan that shows how long different tasks will take and the order they need to be done in.
gelatinisation	When <u>starch</u> particles <u>swell and burst</u>, thickening a liquid.
gelling agent	Something that causes a liquid to thicken or set as a gel.
Genetically Modified (GM) food	Food that's had its genes altered to give it useful characteristics. For example, GM tomatoes that have a longer shelf life than normal.
glazing	Adding a coating to give a product a shiny, glossy appearance.
globalisation	When products grown or produced in one country, are processed and sold all over the world.
gluten	A protein formed when dough is kneaded, that makes the dough <u>stretchy</u>.
Guideline Daily Amounts (GDAs)	<u>How much energy</u> or how much of certain <u>nutrients</u> an average adult needs each day.
HACCP	Hazard Analysis Critical Control Points.
hazard	Anything that could go <u>wrong</u> or cause <u>harm</u>.
heat transference	When heat energy moves from one place to another — by <u>convection</u>, <u>conduction</u> or <u>radiation</u>.
high-risk food	A food in which bacteria can grow quickly.
intensive farming	When animals are reared with <u>little room to move</u>, usually inside. Also called <u>factory farming</u> or <u>battery farming</u>.
job production	Making <u>single</u> products that are <u>unique</u>. Also called <u>craft</u> production.
landfill	A landfill site is a large <u>rubbish dump</u> that's eventually covered over with earth.
life-cycle analysis	A way of working out a product's <u>environmental impacts</u>.
local produce	Food that is produced <u>locally</u>, so doesn't have to be transported as far. Often found at <u>farmers' markets</u>.
marinate	To soak something in a mixture of things before cooking to give it more flavour, e.g. oil, wine, vinegar and herbs.

Glossary

mass production	Making <u>large numbers</u> of a product, often on an assembly line or conveyor belt.
model	A <u>test version</u> of a product that you make during the development stage.
modified starches	Starches that have been <u>treated</u> so that they react in a particular way in certain conditions, e.g. they're used in packet custard to make it thicken instantly. (Modified starches are also called <u>smart starches</u>).
nanoparticles	Very, very, very small particles. Nanoparticles can have different properties, e.g. changing colour at certain temperatures.
nanotechnology	A technology that involves using nanoparticles.
nutrients	Proteins, carbohydrates, fats, vitamins and minerals are all nutrients.
open question	A question that has no set answers, e.g. why don't you like puddings?
organic	Organic crops are grown <u>without</u> using any <u>artificial pesticides</u> or <u>fertilisers</u>. Organic meat is produced to very <u>high welfare standards</u> and <u>without</u> artificial <u>growth hormones</u> or the regular use of <u>antibiotics</u>.
pesticide	A <u>chemical</u> or other substance used to <u>kill pests</u>.
preservative	Something added to food to make it <u>last longer</u>, e.g. adding salt to meat.
preserve	To make food <u>last longer</u> and extend its <u>shelf life</u>.
processed foods	Foods that have been processed in some way, usually for our <u>convenience</u>, e.g. tinned meats. They often have extra <u>salt</u> added so they can be unhealthy.
product specification	A detailed description of how the product should look (including measurements) and taste — it also includes what ingredients will be used.
prototype	The first <u>model</u> of a design idea.
Quality Assurance	Setting and meeting <u>standards</u> for the quality of a product.
Quality Control	Checking that the standards you've set for the quality of a product are being <u>met</u>.
radiation	The transfer of energy through waves of radiation.
raising agent	Something that releases bubbles of gas that expand when heated. Raising agents are used to make cake and dough mixtures rise.
ready meal	A <u>pre-cooked meal</u> that's frozen or chilled — you just need to heat it up.
Recommended Daily Amounts (RDAs)	How much of certain vitamins and minerals an average adult needs each day.

Glossary

recyclable	A recyclable material is one that could be reused fairly easily.
renewable resource	A renewable resource is one that's replaced as fast as it is used up by humans, e.g. softwood trees in a plantation.
resources	Things you need to make new products, e.g. oil is a resource used to make plastic.
risk assessment	Identifying potential hazards and the precautions needed to avoid them.
roux	A sauce base made from plain flour and melted butter.
salmonella	Bacteria that cause food poisoning — often found in eggs and chicken.
saturated fats	A group of fats that come mainly from animal sources and are solid or semi-solid at room temperature.
seasonal foods	Foods that are only produced in a particular season, e.g. British-grown asparagus is only available in May and June.
sensory analysis	Tasting samples of food and rating how good they are in various ways, e.g. taste, texture.
shelf life	The length of time a product can last without going off or losing its quality.
shortening	A fat that's added to a floury mixture to give a product a crumbly texture.
smart materials	Materials that change in certain conditions, e.g. light, temperature etc.
standard food component	A ready-made ingredient or food part, e.g. a ready-made pizza base. They're also called pre-manufactured components.
staple foods	Foods that can be used all year round and make up the main part of people's diets, e.g. bread, rice, pasta and potatoes.
sustainable	A sustainable process or material is one that can be used without causing permanent damage to the environment or completely using up resources, e.g. sustainable wood comes from forests where fast-growing trees are chopped down and replaced.
target group	The group of people you want to sell your product to.
tenderising	Making meat more tender so it's nicer to eat, e.g. by bashing it with a mallet.
unsaturated fats	A group of fats that come mainly from vegetable sources and are usually liquid at room temperature.
work order	A table or a flow chart that shows tasks in sequence.

Answers

Page 5 — Proteins

1) For growth and repair of muscles, tissues and organs, and to help children grow.

2) Three of, e.g. meat / fish / eggs / milk / soya beans.

3) a) Two of, e.g. B vitamins / iron / zinc.
   b) E.g. thiamin (vitamin B1) and niacin (vitamin B3).

4) To tenderise the meat (by partly breaking down the fibres).

5) E.g. white meats still provide lots of protein and B vitamins but they're much lower in saturated fat than red meats.

6) Oily fish, e.g. mackerel. White fish, e.g. cod. Shellfish, e.g. prawns. (Other examples are possible.)

7) Tofu, TVP, Quorn™.

Page 7 — Carbohydrates

1) Sugar, starch and fibre.

2) Granulated sugar — e.g. sweetens tea / put on cereal,
   Caster sugar — e.g. cakes / biscuits,
   Brown sugar — e.g. fruit cakes / gingerbread / Christmas pudding,
   Icing sugar — e.g. icing / sweets.

3) a) It acts as a preservative.
   b) It speeds up fermentation.
   c) It adds sweetness and colour.

4) Any two of, bulking agent (to increase volume), gelling agent (to set things), thickening agent (to thicken things).

5) Smart starches.

Page 9 — Fats, Fibre and Water

1) 1. Butter, made from churning cream.
   2. Margarine, made from blending vegetable oils with other ingredients.
   3. Lard, made from pig fat.
   4. Suet, made from fat around animals' organs.
   5. Oils, made from pressed seeds.
   6. Low-fat spreads, from vegetable oils and water.

2) 1. Butter can be used to add flavour.
   2. Fat mixed with flour helps to shorten pastry, i.e. make it crumbly.
   3. Butter can add colour to pastry.

3) a) Saturated fats come mainly from animal sources, whereas unsaturated fats are mainly from vegetable sources. Also, saturated fats are solid or semi-solid at room temperature, whereas unsaturated fats are liquid.
   b) Saturated fats: any two from, e.g. meat fat / butter / suet / dripping / lard.
      Unsaturated fats: any two from, e.g. sunflower oil / olive oil / rapeseed oil / peanut oil / corn oil / soya oil.
   c) Saturated fat.

4) Any four of, e.g. vegetables, fruit, fruit juice, brown bread, wholemeal/whole grain foods, lentils, beans, seeds, nuts.

5) Soluble and insoluble.

6) You feel thirsty, produce less urine, get headaches, feel faint, get cramp in your muscles, your blood pressure drops, you can fall unconscious, you could become delirious, you could die.

7) Cholesterol, cholesterol, cholesterol, cholesterol, cholesterol, cholesterol, cholesterol, cholesterol, cholesterol, cholesterol, cholesterol, cholesterol, cholesterol, cholesterol, cholesterol, cholesterol [bang].

Page 11 — Vitamins and Minerals

1) Liver, fish, butter, fish oils, eggs and yellow/orange fruit, vegetables and margarine. We need it for good eyesight and healthy tissues.

2) 1. B1, thiamin, is useful because it helps the nervous system and the release of energy from carbohydrates.
   2. B2, riboflavin, is useful because it helps with the release of energy and repair of tissues.
   3. B3, niacin, is useful because it helps with the release of energy.
   4. Folic acid is useful because it's needed for growth. (Other answers are possible.)

3) Vitamin C. It protects the body from infections and allergies, helps us to absorb minerals and helps keep blood vessels healthy and heal wounds.

4) From oily fish and eggs in the diet and from exposure to sunlight. A lack of it can lead to bone diseases, e.g. rickets.

5) a) Any five from, e.g. milk, tofu, salmon, green leafy vegetables, hard water, white bread.
   b) We need it to make our bones and teeth strong, and to keep muscles and nerves healthy.

6) It helps to form haemoglobin, which is needed for healthy blood. It's found in, e.g. spinach and liver.

7) To regulate water content.

8) Any three from, e.g. meat, fish, dairy products, nuts, beans, cereals.

9) Any six from, e.g. vitamin C / vitamin A / B vitamins / dietary fibre / iron / calcium / protein.

10) Fortification.

11) To replace nutrients that are lost during processing or to add extra nutrients to make it healthier.

Page 13 — Cereals, Wheat and Flour

1) Any four from, e.g. wheat, oats, barley, rye, rice, maize, millet.

2) 1. Bran — dietary fibre.
   2. Germ — vitamins and oils.
   3. Endosperm — protein and carbohydrate.

3) a) E.g. pasta.
   b) E.g. biscuits, cakes, porridge.

4) 1. Wholemeal flour — contains all of the grain.
   2. Brown flour — some bran and wheatgerm have been removed, leaving about 85% of the grain.
   3. White flour — most of the bran and wheatgerm have been removed, leaving about 75% of the grain.

5) Wholemeal flour contains all of the wheat grain, which means that none of the bran has been removed so it contains more fibre.

6) Gluten.

7) a) E.g. bread.
   b) E.g. cakes.

8) E.g. yeast, baking powder, bicarbonate of soda. Raising agents release bubbles of gas, which expand when heated and make a mixture rise.

9) Warm chicken and bacon in a garlic & herb marinade, with a lightly dressed salad. Other answers may be acceptable.

Answers

Page 15 — Eggs and Dairy Products

1) Four of e.g. protein, fat, vitamins A, B2 and D, iodine.

2) a) The protein in egg white stretches when it's beaten, trapping air, e.g. in cakes.
   b) Coagulation makes the ingredients stick together, e.g. in burgers.
   c) The egg white coagulates, helping foods set and stay 'thickened', e.g. in quiche.

3) a) The yolk.
   b) Mayonnaise is an emulsion. Egg yolk is used to stop the oily and watery parts of the emulsion separating.

4) Coating/enrobing (for the chicken) and emulsification (for the mayonnaise).

5) E.g. They should always cook eggs thoroughly. They should make sure chicken is cooked properly. They could use dried or pasteurised eggs.

6) Any six of, e.g. protein, fat, carbohydrate, phosphorus, calcium, vitamins A, D and B12.

7) Whole milk, skimmed milk and semi-skimmed milk.

8) E.g. calcium, protein, vitamins A, E, K and some B vitamins.

9) Many silly answers possible.

Page 17 — Food Preparation

1) Foods that can be used all year round and make up the main part of people's diets. Any three examples from, e.g. bread, pastry, rice, pasta, potatoes.

2) Sift flour and salt into a bowl and rub in fat. Mix yeast and warm water together, add to the rest of the ingredients and mix to form a dough. Knead the dough, cover and leave to rest for at least an hour. Shape the dough and bake it.

3) To improve the taste of food / to bring out the flavour of food. Any suitable example, e.g. marinate meat in barbecue marinade before cooking to add flavour to the meat.

4) a) E.g. Use them unpeeled, as the skin is a good source of nutrients.
   b) E.g. Cook them as quickly as possible in a small amount of water.

5) Any three of, e.g. boiled, poached, scrambled, fried.

6) E.g. drain off the fat before serving, use oils with unsaturated fat.

Page 19 — Baking

1) a) Convection, conduction, radiation.
   b) Through convection and radiation, and through the food by conduction.

2) Any two from: food bakes more evenly / the oven heats up quicker and your food cooks quicker / they use less energy.

3) a) Any three reasonable answers, e.g. bread, potatoes, meat.
   b) E.g. It's quite healthy because you don't usually add any extra fat, and fat often leaves food as it's baked, but it can take a long time to bake food.

4) a) Kneading is a method of preparing a product before it's baked, e.g. to make bread. You use your hands to stretch and pull dough — this helps form gluten in the flour, which helps give bread its texture and allows it to rise.
   b) You could use folding when making a cake — you use a spoon or a spatula to fold the mixture in half repeatedly. This stops air being lost when mixing, so helps the cake to rise.
   c) A whisk — used to mix ingredients together and add air, to help products to rise when they're baked.

d) Any two from: you could shape the dough by hand / use a cutter or a knife to cut out the right shape / use a rolling pin to roll out the right shape.

Page 21 — Roasting, Grilling and Frying

1) a) Roasting is done at a higher temperature than baking, so foods cook more quickly and brown more.
   b) Fat can be added to the outside of the food to help it to brown, and stay moist.
   c) Any suitable answer, e.g. a leg of lamb.

2) a) Conduction.
   b) Radiation.
   c) E.g. Food cooks quickly at a high temperature, but this makes it easier to burn the food.

3) a) Stir-frying, shallow frying and deep-fat frying.
   b) E.g. stir-fry — noodles, shallow fry — eggs and deep-fat fry — doughnuts.
   c) Stir-frying because food is cooked quickest using the least amount of oil, so less fat is absorbed by the food.
   d) E.g. It's quicker than roasting / uses less energy.

4) The doughnut has been completely covered in very hot oil or fat / deep-fat fried.

Page 23 — Boiling, Steaming and Microwaving

1) a) Simmering cooks food more gently at a slightly lower temperature.
   b) Through convection (from the liquid to the food) and conduction (through the food).
   c) Boiling is quite a harsh method of cooking and the bubbles would probably break up the fish, so it'd fall apart. You could boil the fish in a bag.
   d) E.g. boiling is quick and no fat is added, so it's quite healthy. But, vegetables lose their colour and nutrients if they're boiled for too long, and food often doesn't taste that nice when it's been boiled.

2) a) Steaming means cooking food with the steam from boiling liquid, not in the liquid itself.
   b) Because no fat is added and vegetables keep more of their nutrients.

3) E.g. microwaves use less energy than a steamer to cook food / microwaving is faster than steaming.

Page 25 — Sauces, Soups and Finishes

1) a) A roux is a sauce base made from butter and flour.
   b) You don't use a sauce base with the all-in-one method — you just add all your ingredients in together.

2) a) Three from e.g. plain flour, cornflour, a roux, potatoes or onions.
   b) E.g. you could add salt, pepper or spices.
   c) A soup is blended to get a smooth consistency but a broth is a liquid with chunks of food in it.

3) E.g. cakes, biscuits, pastries, scones, crumbles.

4) a) E.g. you could add some grated parmesan and black pepper on top of it. You might do this to add extra colour and flavour.
   b) A glaze is a shiny coating applied to the top of food. It's used to make it look shiny and glossy, and more appealing to eat.
   c) E.g. you could decorate the cake with icing, add marzipan figures, etc.

5) Any three from e.g. only boil the amount of water you need / use an appropriate size of pan and ring / cover saucepans and pots with lids / cook different foods together / use the most energy efficient cooking method.

Answers

Page 27 — Healthy Eating

1) 1. Fruit and vegetables. 2. Starchy foods. 3. Dairy foods.
   4. Non-dairy proteins. 5. Fatty/sugary foods.

2) You could look at the product label to check what percentage of the guideline daily amount (GDA) of fat the product provides.

3) Peter meets the eatwell plate guidelines by eating lots of starchy foods, e.g. the wholemeal toast, sandwich bread and rice. He eats some dairy foods, e.g. cheese in his sandwich and his yogurt. He eats some non-dairy sources of protein, e.g. egg in his sandwich and chicken in the curry. But he eats no fruit or vegetables, which he should eat a lot of. He eats far too much sugary and fatty food like jam, a chocolate bar, crisps, chocolate and cake.

4) Eating too much sugar can lead to obesity, type 2 diabetes and tooth decay.

5) Any three of, e.g. reduce the amount of processed and convenience foods you eat, choose foods that are labelled as being low in fat, salt or sugar, modify recipes to make them healthier, add less sugar, salt and fat to your foods.

6) a) Sweetener
   b) E.g. olive oil
   c) Herbs.

Page 29 — Target Groups

1) People with coeliac disease can't eat gluten — so shouldn't have products that contain wheat, barley and rye, e.g. normal bread and pasta. They need to get starch and fibre from other foods e.g. rice and potatoes or from gluten-free alternatives e.g. gluten-free bread.

2) Pregnant women should increase their intake of protein, calcium and iron, and avoid some foods e.g. liver, some cheeses, undercooked meat and alcohol.

3) E.g. making foods 'trendy' (e.g. using celebrity endorsements) or using special offers to promote particular products.

4) People might choose to buy e.g. free-range, organic, fair trade, local or sustainable products, and avoid e.g. endangered products.

Page 31 — Changing Trends

1) Globalisation is the improvement of trade and transport links which means goods can be produced in one country, and processed and sold all over the world. It means there is a wider variety of exotic foods available for us to eat because they can be easily transported from far away countries.

2) Manufacturers developed frozen products and microwavable meals.

3) Food scares are when health problems are linked to particular foods.

4) Providing enough resources without damaging or destroying the environment or using up limited resources.

5) E.g. forest clearing and soil erosion.

6) A resource that never runs out.

7) E.g. solar power

Page 33 — The 6Rs

1) Recycle, reuse, reduce, refuse, rethink and repair.

2) Any three of, e.g. steel/ aluminium , plastic, glass, card, paper.

3) Biodegradable materials rot naturally in the environment, so they don't take up space in landfill.

4) a) E.g. use stale bread to make bread-and-butter pudding
   b) E.g. use sugar beet waste to feed pigs.

5) E.g. cod isn't sustainable — replace it with pollack.

6) Refuse — she should refuse the product with excess packaging.

7) Refuse, rethink, repair and reduce.

8) Sugar, salt and fat.

9) E.g. vitamin C, folic acid.

Page 35 — Choosing Ingredients

1) Advantages: any two of, e.g. saves time, saves money, less machinery needed, fewer specialist skills needed, safer and more hygienic, products are more consistent.
   Disadvantages: any two of, e.g. you can't pick and choose or alter components, not always reliable, might not be as tasty, takes up space, may need extra packaging and transport.

2) Any three of, e.g. pizza bases, pastry, cake mixes, bread mixes, fillings, sauces, icing, marzipan.

3) E.g. make soups from odd-shaped vegetables that can't be sold, use chicken bones or vegetable scraps to make stock.

Page 37 — Morals and Ethics

1) Animals don't waste energy moving or keeping warm because as many animals as possible are kept in the available space. So all their energy goes into food production.

2) Growth hormones speed up growth, making it quicker and cheaper to produce meat.

3) Free-range products come from animals that are free to roam.

4) Less food can be produced, so it's more expensive.

5) a) A scheme to help workers in LEDCs get a fair price for their produce and good working conditions.
   b) Advantages: any one of, e.g. farmers and workers are treated fairly, help workers to invest in their communities, workers have a better quality of life.
   Disadvantages: e.g. excess food causes world prices to fall, so those not in a fair trade scheme might lose out.

6) Fair trade helps communities to build schools, health centres etc.

7) a) Ethical Trade Initiative
   b) It's tries to ensure that all workers are paid fair wages and are protected by health and safety laws. It also tries to make people more aware of the working conditions of some workers that make cheap products.

8) To get to the other side. Other answers acceptable.

Page 39 — Organic and GM Foods

1) Chemical or other substance used to control pests.

2) E.g. damages the environment, harmful to people.

3) Any three of, e.g. introduce natural predators, crop rotation, biological pesticides, spraying crops with hot water.

4) A food that is produced 'naturally' (i.e. without the use of chemicals) and to really high animal welfare standards.

5) Animals and crops take longer to grow, crops aren't sprayed with chemicals to protect them so more are lost.

Answers

6) Genetically Modified

7) Advantages: any two of, e.g. crops grow quickly, more crops are produced, crops are cheaper, they have a longer shelf life, less is wasted, foods are available all year round.
Disadvantages: any two of, e.g. long-term health effects aren't known, modified genes could get into the wider environment, can't be sold everywhere.

8) Some people believe it's not natural to mess around with genes and the long-term health effects aren't known.

Page 41 — Packaging and the Environment

1) Any three of, e.g. to contain the product neatly / to protect the product from damage when it's transported/displayed / to preserve the food / to avoid contamination / to identify what the product is / to give customers useful information

2) E.g. it can't be hazardous to human health, it can't make food go off, it can't cause an unacceptable change in quality.

3) a) Advantages — e.g. it's strong and rigid / it's transparent so customers can see the product / it's resistant to high temperatures / it can be reused and recycled.
Disadvantages — e.g. it's pretty heavy / it breaks easily.
   b) Advantages — e.g. they're strong / they're resistant to high temperatures / it can be recycled.
Disadvantages — e.g. metals can react with some foods / customers can't see the contents / they are a finite resource.

4) A microwavable plastic.

5) Any three of, e.g. uses energy and can use non-renewable resources, excess packaging uses extra resources to make, packaging used once then thrown away which takes up space in waste dumps, some packaging doesn't biodegrade.

6) Any two of, e.g. recycle tins, plastic, glass, card and paper, buy products with little or no packaging, choose products with biodegradable packaging, choose products with packaging made from recycled materials.

7) Increase the amount of packaging that can be recycled, reduce the amount of packaging in total.

Page 43 — Transport and Labelling

1) Transporting foods burns fossil fuels, which produce gases that add to global warming.

2) a) The distance food travels from where it's produced to where it's sold.
   b) Buy local products from farmers' markets.

3) A measure of the impact your life has on the environment in terms of the amount of green house gases produced.

4) A measure of how you use the planet's resources against how much waste you produce.

5) Any five of, e.g. product name and what it is, weight / volume, storage instructions, best before / use by date, manufacturer's name and address, country of origin (if the consumer might be mislead), cooking instructions, ingredients.

6) When they make a special nutritional claim.

7) E.g. suitable for vegetarians, possible allergy problems, traffic-light labelling.

Page 45 — Design and Research

1) Because they need to make sure they're making a product that people really want.

2) It explains why there's a need for a new product — it gives information about the context, who it involves, why the product is needed and how it will be used. The design brief is important because it's the starting point for the development of the product.

3) a) The group of people you want to sell your product to.
   b) Any reasonable answers, e.g. gender, age, job, hobbies, lifestyle, income, etc.
   c) Any five sensible answers, e.g. you could ask about age, job, favourite fruits and/or vegetables, whether they like salad dressings, where/when they eat salads, etc.

4) Any sensible answers, e.g.
   a) Do you like cheese in your sandwiches?
   b) What kind of fillings do you like?
   c) Which of the following types of bread do you like? White, brown, wholemeal, rye.

Page 47 — Analysis

1) Taking a product apart and examining what it's made from and how it's put together etc. (Or similar answer.)

2) Any three reasonable answers, e.g. price, ingredients, nutritional information, ideas about the target market, storage/cooking instructions, etc.

3) Any five reasonable answers, e.g. poor quality ingredients, unpleasant taste, smell, texture or flavour, poor quality packaging, poor nutritional value, too expensive.

4) To rate which foods taste / smell / look best. Or to find out what consumers think about new or existing products. A common test is a rating or ranking test.

5) a) The colour and texture (and possibly size).
   b) The smell and the taste.

Page 49 — Design Specification

1) A list of design criteria / requirements that say what the product should be like.

2) E.g. the dessert should:
   • be sweet and chocolate flavoured.
   • be low in calories.
   • have a fairly solid texture.

3) Work from an existing product, use brainstorming.
(Other answers are possible.)

4) a) Compare them with the design specification, decide which ones are good and sketch and annotate them.
   b) Do a freehand sketch. (Other answers are possible.)
   c) By checking which one most closely matches the design criteria.

Page 51 — Development

1) Making different versions of a product to test and evaluate.

2) Any two reasonable answers, e.g. change the proportions of ingredients, change the cooking method.

3) Any two sensible suggestions, e.g. try a different kind of dough for the pizza base, use fresher toppings, add olive oil.

4) Because then your product probably wouldn't meet the design brief.

Answers

Page 53 — Planning Production

1) A description of what the product contains, how it looks, tastes, etc.

2) The design specification.

3) a) It helps to plan each task in sequence.
   b) It helps to plan the timing of tasks.

4) Answers should look something like the following:

   a)

   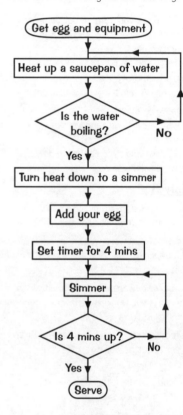

   b)

   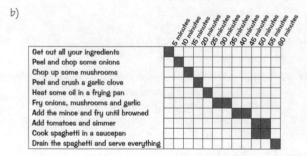

5) You should test it to make sure it meets the design specification. You may also want to use more questionnaires and surveys, and record your findings. (Other answers are possible.)

Page 55 — Different Types of Production

1) Any two differences, e.g. job production makes a single product, mass production makes a large number; job production uses an individual recipe or method, mass production uses a production line; job production is quite expensive and takes a long time, mass production is cheap and quick; job production needs workers with specialist skills, mass production uses unskilled workers.

2) a) Batch production — because lots of sandwiches can be made in one go so it's quick, and you can change between making batches of different kinds of sandwiches.
   b) Job production / craft production.

3) a) Non-stop production / production 24 hours a day.
   b) It keeps production costs per product really low for products that are sold in large numbers.
   c) E.g. it's very expensive to set up because very specialised equipment is needed / if anything goes wrong, it takes time to get it going again and unproductive time costs money.
   d) Computer-aided manufacture.
   e) Any two from, e.g. production costs are lower / production is quicker / staff don't need to handle food as much so it's more hygienic / the product will be more consistent.

4) They can use CAD to produce 2D and 3D images of the product and its packaging. Once the product's been drawn on screen the design can easily be changed and values recalculated, and it's much quicker and more accurate than re-drawing designs on paper.

Page 57 — Shelf Life and Packaging

1) A use by date is a safety warning and is used on products with a short shelf life. If you eat food after this date, it might be dangerous. A best before date is a quality warning and is used on products with a longer shelf life. If you eat food after this date, it'll probably be safe but might not be as nice.

2) Any three of, e.g. sickness, diarrhoea, stomach cramps, fever.

3) E.g. E. coli, salmonella, listeria.

4) Moisture, warmth, neutral pH.

5) They're moist and high in protein.

6) Any four of, e.g. meat, fish, poultry, dairy products, eggs, gravies, stocks, sauces, shellfish, seafood, cooked rice.

7) a) Modified Atmosphere Packaging (MAP).
   b) The food is put into plastic packaging with a mixture of oxygen, nitrogen and carbon dioxide in specific proportions. It's then sealed and chilled.

8) a) Any two of, e.g. fresh meat, cooked meat, fresh pasta, cheese, sandwiches.
   b) Any two of, e.g. coffee, meat, fish.
   c) Any two of, e.g. baked beans, cooked meats, soup.

9) E.g. adding clay nanoparticles makes the packaging better at keeping out oxygen and moisture, some nanoparticles can kill harmful bacteria, smart packaging can indicate a change in conditions.

Answers

Page 59 — Preservation and Additives

1) Food is cooked then chilled to between 0 °C and 5 °C within 90 minutes. It's kept in a fridge, then reheated (to above 72 °C).

2) The range of temperatures that bacteria grow and multiply very quickly in — between 5 °C and 63 °C.

3) -18 °C.

4) a) Salt absorbs water from bacteria, making them shrivel up and die.
   b) Vinegar is too acidic for bacteria to grow in.

5) Any three of, e.g. some people are allergic or react badly to some additives, some additives in large quantities can be bad for your health, they can disguise poor quality ingredients.

Page 61 — Tools and Equipment

1) a) Weighing scales/cup.
   b) Measuring jug/cup.

2) Slicing/cutting foods evenly.

3) Any three of, e.g. hand, spoon, whisk, mixer, blender, food processor, floor-standing mixer.

4) They won't be consistent / they'll be different shapes and sizes.

5) A mould.

6) Any four of, e.g. ovens, hobs, microwaves, steamers, tunnel ovens, deck ovens, travel ovens.

7) Checking the inside temperature of food to make sure it's been cooked properly.

8) Industrial ovens are larger and will often be computer-controlled.

9) a) Cutting things.
   b) Mixing, slicing, chopping or dicing.
   c) Shaping.
   d) Steaming/cooking things.

10) It's quicker and gives consistent results.

11) You get consistent results, it's quicker and easier, measurements are more accurate.

12) It'll hurt, you might lose a finger and it'll be very messy.

Page 63 — Safety and Quality Checking

1) Cross-contamination is when bacteria are passed from one thing to another.

2) a) Follow personal hygiene procedures (wash hands, wear a clean apron, wear a hat or hair net, remove jewellery, cover cuts, report illness, don't taste food with your fingers), use clean equipment to avoid cross-contamination, defrost food thoroughly before cooking.
   b) Transport food quickly and securely and at the right temperature, avoid cross-contamination by transporting raw and cooked food separately, keep equipment clean.

3) An EHO maintains and improves public health standards, by checking food hygiene, making sure health and safety regulations are being followed, checking food storage, preparation and sale areas are clean and safe, and that food is safe to eat.

4) Quality Assurance is about setting standards and meeting them. Quality Control is checking that the standards are being met.

Page 65 — HACCP

1) a) Anything that could cause harm or problems when making, packaging, storing or transporting the product.
   b) The likelihood of a hazard causing a problem.
   c) Thinking about what problems could happen, when they could happen and what the steps are to reduce the risk of them happening.

2) Hazard Analysis Critical Control Points. Manufacturers use it to identify potential hazards and prevent food from being contaminated.

3) Biological contamination, chemical contamination, physical contamination.

4) You can avoid biological contamination by testing samples of each product for contamination. You can avoid chemical contamination by storing cleaning fluids etc. away from food. You can avoid physical contamination by wearing overalls and hairnets, not wearing jewellery and keeping food covered.

5) Think about your product from field to table and identify any potential hazards at each step. Then think about how to control and prevent the hazards you have identified.

Index

Index

Index